THIRTEEN LESSONS
ON ISLAM
FOR CHRISTIANS

A SELF STUDY COURSE—
THE SECOND LEVEL

THIRTEEN LESSONS
ON ISLAM
FOR CHRISTIANS

A SELF STUDY COURSE—
THE SECOND LEVEL

V 02.28.08

PUBLISHED BY CSPI, LLC

WWW.CSPIPUBLISHING.COM

PRINTED IN THE USA

TABLE OF CONTENTS

INTRODUCTION

The average person knows more about atomic physics than he does about Islam. But now, for the first time in history, the ordinary person can learn the truth about Islam.

In the past, we have only known what scholars say. Ordinary people never could understand Islam for themselves. That has changed. If you work your way through these simple lessons, you will be able to make sense of the news and what people say and write.

You will be able to talk and reason about Islam and make your point. You will be authoritative because what you know is based on the actual doctrine of Islam. You will know the same material that the imam (Islamic leader) uses. After learning the actual doctrine of Islam, you will realize that the media's explanation about Islam is based upon ignorance.

The media only report what Islam does but never "why" they do what they do. After these lessons, you will know why Muslims act and speak as they do. You will also be able to predict the future and see how wrong our policies about Islam are. Our politics are based upon a profound ignorance of Islamic doctrine and history.

Most of what you will study is politics, not religion. Islam is a political system similar to communism with a god. It is not the religion that concerns us. September 11, 2001, was a political act with a religious motive. Islam's strength is its politics, not its religion. Do you really care about how a Muslim prays? No, what difference does that make to you? But the Sharia law they want to implement will dictate to you how you live your life, what you can say, read, and write. Religion is personal, Sharia law is control of all public space—education, art, law, the media, dress, customs and more, and all must submit to Islamic law. Islamic politics is pure oppression. Islam means "submit" and you will submit or die. That is politics, not religion.

To show how important Islamic politics is in comparison to the religion, consider the fact that Mohammed preached the religion of Islam for 13 years in Mecca and garnered only 150 followers. When he turned to war and politics, he conquered all of Arabia in 10 years. Not even Mohammed could make the religion of Islam succeed on its own.

Every Muslim is a Mohammedan. A Muslim has to worship Allah exactly like Mohammed and live like Mohammed. He is the key to Islam, not Allah. You will learn about Mohammed's life and how he went from being an orphan to being the first king of Arabia.

Many people have a fear or dread about learning about Islam. It seems so hard. After all, nobody seems to actually know anything about it. People may fear Islam, but they do not know any facts.

Here is the good news. Islam is fascinating, because it is so different from anything you have ever studied. You may have heard Islam compared to Christianity. Nothing could be further from the truth. If there are a hundred ways to compare Islam and Christianity, then they are similar on about 3 points out of a 100.

Since we have almost ignored Islam for the past 1400 years, the English language has never agreed on how to spell the words of Islam. Examples: Moslem, Muslim; Mohammed, Muhammad; Quran, Koran and so forth. This confusion is the price of ignorance.

This book is part of a self-study course. It can be used by itself in a class studying Islam, or it can be used along with *A Guide to Islam for Christians* and *Thirteen Talks on Islam* (an audio book) as a complete self-study course. The *Guide* is a mini-encyclopedia of Islam and is keyed to the *Thirteen Lessons*. The *Guide* is also a teacher's aid.

The recommended order for self-study is:

Thirteen Talks on Islam, Level 1
Thirteen Lessons on Islam for Christians, Level 2
A Guide to Islam for Christians, Level 3

There are two ways to study this series. The first is to listen to the talk on slavery, for example, then read the lesson on slavery. After that you can study the slavery chapter in the *Guide*.

The other method is to listen to all the talks, read all of the *Lessons* and then the read the *Guide*. It is your choice.

This book is also available without the audio book and is suitable as a lesson book in a Sunday school class.

MAP OF
ARABIA
600 A.D.

MEDITER-
RANEAN
SEA

SYRIA

MESOPOTAMIA
(IRAQ)

•Muta

•Tabuk

•Fadak
•Khaybar

ARABIA

•Medina

•Badr

•Mecca
•Hudabiya
•Hunain

EGYPT

RED SEA

YEMEN

N

ABYSSINIA
(ETHIOPIA)

MOHAMMED

Lesson 1

SUMMARY

- Islam is entirely based upon Mohammed. The easiest and surest way to know Islam is to study Mohammed's life and words.

- Mohammed was born in Mecca 1400 years ago. He was an orphan who became a business man. At about 40 years of age he started to have visions and hear voices. The voice told him that he was a prophet of Allah. He began to tell others of his message from Allah. After 13 years the Meccans ran him out of town and he moved to Medina.

- In Medina he became a politician and war leader. He developed jihad, sacred violence for Allah. Over the next 10 years Mohammed crushed his enemies and became the first ruler of all Arabia. He destroyed most of the Jews and Christians in the process.

- We know the smallest details of the way he ate, his anger, his appearance and even his family life.

A NOTE

In this book, the words Christian and Christianity are used in a general sense and do not refer to any particular church. Although Christians are used to distinguishing among themselves, to Muslims all churches are the same.

MOHAMMED'S LIFE

The life of Mohammed is as important to Muslims as the life of Christ is to Christians. The Koran says more than 70 times that Muslims are to copy Mohammed's life in the smallest detail. Every Muslim is a Mohammedan. They do not worship Mohammed, but they imitate him in every aspect of life from worship to bathroom habits. Over 75% of the Muslim "Bible" is about Mohammed, not Allah.

MOHAMMED'S LIFE

Mohammed was born in 570 AD in Mecca in Arabia. He was born into an upper class clan but became an orphan and was raised by his uncle. His uncle was a trader and taught Mohammed the business of going to Syria and bringing back goods to sell in Mecca. He married a successful older widow, Khadija.

Mohammed had a religious mind and inquired about Christianity and Judaism on his business trips to Syria. Syria was north of Arabia and bordered the Mediterranean Sea and was Christian and part of the Byzantine Empire.

At that time, Arabia had Jews in the northern part and a few Christians scattered about the area. The great majority of Arabians were polytheists. Many tribes or towns had their own deity. When one person married another, both deities would be worshipped. Mecca was a religious pilgrimage site with a shrine called the Kabah. The Kabah was a stone building shaped like a cube. A picture of Jesus and Mary was inside, along with symbols of 360 gods.

Mohammed had religious retreats in a cave near Mecca. When he was about 40, he had a vision from an angel he later called Gabriel. This was the beginning of visions and visitations reported by Mohammed. At first the god of Gabriel had no name. Later this god had the name Allah.

The Koran never explains who Allah is, and for a good reason. Allah was the god of the Quraysh tribe, Mohammed's tribe. Mohammed's father was named Abdullah (meaning, slave of Allah). His other brothers were named after other Arabic gods. The Quraysh were the overseers of the Kabah and was in charge of pilgrimages. The Quraysh were similar to the priestly tribe of the Levites. Allah was the moon god of the Quraysh and was the chief god of the many gods in Mecca. Mohammed promoted Allah from chief god to the only god.

PROPHET

Mohammed began to tell his friends and family about his visions and recited the poetry of the early Koran that he said came from the angel Gabriel. Some languages are easier to write poetry in than others, and Arabic is given to easy poetry (but is very poor at precise language). Later Mohammed preached his doctrine to all of Mecca. At first, the Meccans did not care one way or the other about Mohammed's preaching. They had 360 religions and another one was fine with them.

Mohammed preached the doctrine of a Judgment Day and that all of the Arabians who had already died were going to go to Hell. This enraged the Meccans. An Arabian's ancestry was of critical importance to them and to be told that their ancestors were going to Hell was too much. Mohammed was aggressive with his message and went every day to the market place and the Kabah and argued with anyone and everyone. Mohammed insulted and demeaned the Meccans. Mecca was in turmoil about Islam.

Medina

After 13 years of preaching, Mohammed had gained only 150 followers. The religion of Islam was not a success. The Meccans drove Mohammed and all of the Muslims out of town, and they went to Medina, about a hundred miles north. Islam calls this the Immigration; those who left were called the Immigrants.

The event is so important that the Islamic calendar started on this date. The Arabic word for immigration is *haj,* also *hajj,* so the Islamic calendar is AH (anno haj). One of the Five Pillars of Islam is the pilgrimage to Mecca, the Haj. The immigrant is a sacred figure and the first stage of jihad is immigration.

After being in Medina for a year, the Muslims were very poor, and Mohammed made the most important decision of his life. He sent out armed raiders to try to steal from the Meccan caravans that passed Medina. On the eighth try, they succeeded and returned with the stolen goods and Meccans captives to be ransomed.

Mohammed was generous with money, and he shared the wealth with all of the Muslims. Suddenly, Islam changed from being a religion to being a political system with a war policy called jihad. Islam became the religion that paid and paid well. His followers increased to 250.

Jihad

Apologists for Islam depict Mohammed as being forced into war as a defensive act. As a measure of this, his first success came after 8 failed attempts, in which his raiders left Medina to seek out Meccan caravans. It is critical to understand that for Islam, all jihad is defensive. It is the unbeliever who offends Allah by denying Islam. Therefore, all Islamic violence is defensive. If the Meccans had believed Mohammed and not offended Allah, then he would not have been forced to kill them.

Mohammed went from small raids on caravans to open combat against Meccan armies. The entire nature of the Koran changed. In Mecca about two-thirds of the Koran raged about those who did not believe Mohammed and condemned all of them to Hell. But later in Medina, the Koran spoke of the sword, captives, enslavement, ransoms and war booty. Allah called all Muslims to jihad against those who did not believe Mohammed.

The Jews

Most of the jihad had been against the Arabs. However, after Mohammed had settled scores against the Arabs, he turned to the Jews. In Mecca the Koran was filled with Jewish stories that had been retold to prove that Mohammed was the last in the line of Jewish prophets. Indeed, the claim was that the Jewish prophets had really been Muslims and the Old Testament had been corrupted to cover the Islamic nature of the message from god.

The Koran from Mecca also claimed that the god of the Jews was Allah. In short, Mohammed made liberal use of the Jewish scriptures. Key to all of this is that very few Jews lived in Mecca, so no one contradicted him.

However, in Medina, half of the citizens were Jews, and they did not accept Mohammed as a prophet. The Koran then turned on the Jews and condemned them to Hell.

After the Koran cursed the Jews in Medina, Mohammed annihilated the three Jewish tribes one at a time. The Jews of Medina were separated by their own hatreds of each other and would not support each other in war.

Then he struck out against Jews who lived a hundred miles away. In the end, every non-Muslim in Arabia was exiled, murdered, enslaved or made a semi-slave called a *dhimmi* [more about dhimmis later].

Triumph

Ten years after he was exiled, Mohammed returned to Mecca as its conqueror. His first order of business was to pray at the Kabah[1]. Then he issued death warrants for every person who had opposed him, including two dancing girls who had sung a song satirizing him. He also had one of his previous secretaries executed. The secretary had begun to suspect that Mohammed was making up the Koran revelations and left Islam and fled Medina to Mecca. Mohammed killed anyone who spoke against him.

All of Arabia became Islamic, and Mohammed became the first ruler of all of Arabia.

---

1   The Kabah is a stone building in Mecca, roughly a 30 foot on edge cube. It is the direction that all Muslims pray towards. There is no Islam without the Kabah.

Mohammed was involved with an event of violence on the average of every 6 weeks for 9 years and that does not include assassinations, Muslims forcing themselves on women[2], and executions.

THE TRADITIONS OF MOHAMMED

There are many small stories about Mohammed called traditions or hadith. These are all sacred writings since a Muslim is to copy Mohammed in all things. Each of the stories has a number similar to chapter-verse of the Bible. The next chapter will explain more about hadiths. For now, Bukhari and Abu Muslim are the two chief writers of hadiths.

His Anger

There are many hadiths about Mohammed's anger. His example is why so many Muslims are easily angered.

> Bukhari 8,73,130 *There was once a curtain with pictures of animals on it in my [Aisha's] house. When Mohammed saw it, his face became flushed with anger. He tore it to bits and said, "People that paint such pictures will receive Hell's most terrible punishment on Judgment Day."*

Muslims are given to cursing their enemies, just like Mohammed.

> Bukhari 9,85,73 *Mohammed would beseech Allah in this prayer, "Allah, Save the weak Muslims. Be cruel to the Mudar tribe and smite them with years of famine and hunger just as you brought famine to the people during the time of Joseph."*

Here we see how Mohammed used characters from the Old Testament. Everything about Islam, except jihad, came from Judaism, Christianity, the tribal religions of Arabia and Zoroasterism. But the ideas were not just borrowed, but changed to show that Mohammed was a prophet.

Wives

Mohammed had about eleven wives[3] and several slaves used for pleasure. Aisha was his favorite wife. Mohammed dreamt of his favorite wife, Aisha, when she was six and he was in his early fifties.

> Muslim 031,5977 *Aisha quotes Mohammed: "Three nights in a row I saw you in a dream. An angel delivered you wrapped in silks*

---

2 Islam has a very detailed doctrine of how women are to be treated. Since this book is to be used in churches, very modest language is used for horrible acts.
3 Oddly enough, there are different reports about the numbers of wives.

and said, 'This is your wife.' As I unwrapped the silk, your face appeared. I said, 'If this dream is indeed from Allah, then let Him make it happen.'"

His marriage [he was 53 upon consummation]:

> Bukhari 7,62,65 *Mohammed and Aisha were married when she was six. They consummated the marriage when she was nine. Hisham said, "I was told that Aisha stayed with Mohammed from the age of nine until his death."*

Aisha in the harem:

> Bukhari 8,73,151 *My girl friends and I [Aisha] would play with dolls while in Mohammed's presence. They would try to hide when he entered, but he always would call them back to play with me. Playing with dolls or anything with a human image was forbidden, but because I was so young, not yet having reached puberty, it was allowed.*

Habits

Islam consists of external behavior that copies Mohammed.

> Bukhari 7,65,292 *Mohammed preferred to begin things from the right side; combing his hair, putting on his shoes, or performing ablution[1]. He would follow this practice in every thing he did.*

> Muslim 023,5018 *Anas said that Mohammed forbade people to drink while standing. Qatada related: We asked him, "What about eating while standing?" Anas said, "That is even more objectionable."*

> Muslim 023,5029 *Anas related the story that Mohammed would drink his refreshments in three gulps.*

> Muslim 023,5037 *Mohammed: "When a Muslim eats, they should not wipe their hand until it is licked clean, either by themselves or by someone else."*

> Muslim 024,5231 *Mohammed: "When someone puts on sandals, he should put the right one on first. When someone takes off sandals, he should take off the left one first. Either this or simply put them on or take them off at the same time."*

> Muslim 024,5234 *Mohammed made it illegal for a man to eat with his left hand or walk with only one sandal on. He also forbade*

---

1   Ablution is ritual cleansing with water.

a man to wear a garment that had no opening for the arms to extend or support himself when wearing a single garment that might expose his privates.

The world is supposed to imitate Mohammed in the smallest acts.

Muslim 024,5238 *Mohammed: "No one should lie on his back with one foot placed on top of the other."*

Mohammed seems to have been exceptionally modest.

Bukhari 7,72,807 *One day a man peeped into Mohammed's house and saw him scratching his head with a comb. Noticing the man Mohammed said, "If I had realized that you were peeking at me I would have stuck this comb in your eye. The reason that people must ask permission is to keep them from seeing things that they shouldn't."*

Humor in jihad.

Muslim 031,5932 *Saed reported, on the authority of his father, that Allah's Apostle gathered his parents for him on the Day of Uhud when a kafir[2] had attacked the Muslims. Thereupon Allah's Apostle said to him: "(Saed), shoot an arrow, may my mother and father be taken as ransom for you." I drew an arrow and I shot a featherless arrow at the Meccan kafir, aiming at his side. He fell down and his private parts were exposed. Allah's Messenger laughed so that I saw his front teeth.*

When you read about Islamic cruelty to non-Muslims, here is one reason Muslims are cruel.

Bukhari 2,24,577 *Some people came to Medina and submitted to Islam, but the climate made them sick, so Mohammed gave them permission to stay among the camels that had been collected for taxes. He told them to drink the camel's urine and milk, as that would cure their illness. However, the people instead murdered Mohammed's slave shepherd and stole the camels. Mohammed sent men after them and they were quickly captured. Mohammed ordered that their hands and feet be cut off (and cauterized, so they would not bleed to death), and their eyes pierced with hot pokers. They were left to die of thirst on the rocks of Harra.*

---

2 A kafir is a non-Muslim. The Koran says that a kafir may be killed, stolen from, tortured, violated, deceived, beheaded, crucified, and abused. Allah hates the kafir and a Muslim is to never be a friend to a kafir.

Here are two of the many hadiths that report Mohammed's whiteness. Interestingly enough, Muslims tell blacks that Islam is the religion of the black man.

> Bukhari 4,56,765 *When Mohammed prostrated himself to pray, he would spread his arms so wide apart, that we could see his armpits. Ibn Bukair described it as "the whiteness of his armpits."*

> Bukhari 1,3,63 *We were sitting with Mohammed in the Mosque one day when a man rode up on a camel. He asked, "Which one of you is Mohammed?" We answered, "That white man leaning on his arm..."*

AFTER MOHAMMED

After Mohammed died, a new leader had to be chosen. He did not appoint anyone to succeed him, nor did he leave any process to choose a new leader. Abu Bakr, Mohammed's closest companion, was selected to be the caliph, a combination of pope and king. After Mohammed's death, many of the new Muslims wanted to leave Islam. However, being an apostate (leaving Islam) call for a death sentence, and Abu Bakr spent the next two years killing all of those who wanted to leave.

After his death, Umar, another of Mohammed's Companions (Companions are similar to the Apostles and disciples), became caliph. Umar spent the next ten years in a violent jihad against Egypt, Syria, Iraq and Persia. Christianity was destroyed in these areas. A Persian he had enslaved killed Umar.

The next caliph was Uthman, another Companion of Mohammed. He reigned for twelve years and was killed by Abu Bakr's grandson over a political dispute. Uthman's body was put on the town dump.

Ali was the last of the Companions of Mohammed to be caliph. His reign was all about internal politics. He was implicated as part of the conspiracy that assassinated Uthman. Aisha, Mohammed's favorite wife, led a civil war against Ali. In the end, Ali was killed. In what was to become a source of the Sunni/Shia[1] split, his two sons were killed as well.

Abu Bakr was the only one of Mohammed's Companions who became caliph and died a natural death. The die of Islam was cast.

---

1   The split between the Sunnis and the Shias is primarily religious. For the unbeliever, the split is of no consequence. Both Sunni and Shia treat the unbeliever the same way.

QUESTIONS

What is the surest and easiest way to know Islam?

Why is every Muslim a Mohammedan?

Why did Mohammed have to leave Mecca?

Why can it be said that Mohammed was a failure as a prophet?

Many Muslims anger easily. Why?

Cruelty can be a virtue in Islam. Why?

How have you seen cruelty in the news?

What do you find to be the most unusual trait in Mohammed?

Why is the Iranian legal age for marriage nine years of age for a girl?

Some Muslims say that Mohammed was forced into violence. What do you think?

THE BASICS OF ISLAM

Lesson 2

SUMMARY

- The Koran is what Mohammed says are the words of Allah. Many of the stories from the Old Testament are retold to support the Islamic belief that Mohammed is the last in the line of Jewish prophets and other prophets of Allah.

- The Koran defines who Allah is. Allah is to be feared, not loved. Allah determines all that happens and hates the unbelievers.

- The Hadith contains the details of how Mohammed is the model Muslim in all that he did and said. The Sira contains his entire life story.

- There is both a religious Islam and a political Islam.

KNOWING ISLAM

Islam is usually held to be nearly impossible to understand, but that is no longer true.

We forget that at one time Christian doctrine was obscure and was known only to scholars. Literacy was rare. One of the most important events in history was the publishing of the King James Bible. Knowledge that had been hidden was put into the hands of the common man. Once the Bible had been translated, Christianity "invented" universal education so that all people could read the Bible. This was the first time in humanity's history that the common man was taught to read and write.

That same thing has been recently done for Islam. The "Bible" of Islam has been put into a form so that anyone can understand the doctrine of Islam. If you stay the course and finish these thirteen lessons, you will become "literate" about Islam.

When you finish this study, you will know the language of Islam and be able to instruct others. You will see the news in a new light and understand how little our leaders and the media know almost nothing about Islam. You will know the answer to what is the real Islam?

There is only one real way to know Islam. Let's start with what every Muslim in the world agrees on. To be a Muslim you must say, "There is no god but Allah and Mohammed is his prophet." That statement tells us the foundation of Islam. The words of Allah, Mohammed's god, are only found in the Koran. But the Koran says over 70 times that all Muslims should imitate Mohammed in every aspect of life. But how do we know how to imitate Mohammed? What Mohammed did and said (called the Sunna) is recorded in great detail. We know more about Mohammed than we know about George Washington.

THE ISLAMIC BIBLE—THE TRILOGY

Islam is defined as three things: the words of Allah, the Koran, and the words and actions of Mohammed.

The words and actions of Mohammed, called the Sunna, are found in two collections of texts—the Sira (Mohammed's life) and the Hadith. His words and actions are considered to be the divine pattern for humanity acceptable to Allah.

A hadith, also called a tradition, is a brief story about what Mohammed did or said. A collection of hadiths is called a Hadith. [It is a little confusing.] There are collections of hundreds of thousands of hadiths, but most of them are not reliable. As an example, we know from the Koran that Mohammed never performed any miracles. But many of the hadiths are filled with miracles.

Those by Bukhari and Abu Muslim are accepted by all Muslims to be "gospel". So the Trilogy is:

- The Koran
- The Sira or biographies by Ishaq and Al Tabari
- The Hadith or Traditions by Bukhari and Abu Muslim

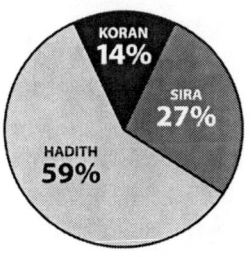

The Islamic "Bible"

The Trilogy is the foundation of Islam. All biographies of Mohammed are based upon the Sira and Hadith. All of Islamic law, the Sharia, is based upon the Trilogy. Every statement and action of political and religious Islam come from the Trilogy.

The Koran is compared wrongly to the Bible. The Koran is only 14% of Islam's sacred texts and does not contain nearly enough information to tell someone how to be a Muslim. The Muslim Bible would be the Koran, the Sira and the Hadith. The Koran is similar to the Torah, the first five books of the Old Testament. The Sira compares to the Gospels and the Hadith has similarities to the Letters.

Measured by the textual doctrine, Islam is 86% Mohammed and 14% Allah. But since Mohammed is the only person who ever "heard" from Allah, the Koran is really about Mohammed. So Islam is 100% Mohammed.

WHAT IS THE KORAN?

Islam believes that the Koran is the perfect, eternal, universal, and final word of the only god, Allah. The Koran does not have the slightest error. It was brought by Mohammed who is the ideal pattern for all behavior of all peoples for all times, now and forever.

The *Koran* (Qur'an, Quran) means, "recitation" and is put together in suras (chapters). Muslims say the Koran was at the right hand of Allah from the beginning of the world, written on emerald tablets in heaven and was revealed to Mohammed in visions by Allah through Gabriel, an angel.

The Koran is extremely repetitive. The story of Moses is told 39 times, for instance. It took twenty-three years to compile. When Mohammed died there was no such thing as a Koran as we know it. It was written down on everything from paper to shoulder bones. Mostly, it was memorized. Only after Mohammed's death was there any attempt to write it all down. The version we have now was put together by the third Caliph, Uthman, about 60 years after Mohammed's death. All source documents were burned after the Koran was compiled. Muslims brag that there are no variant versions of the Koran (not really true)[1].

The Koran was the first book ever written in Arabia. Only poems and business correspondence had been written in Arabic before. Mohammed mentioned "People of the Book" many times, referring to Jews and Christians and the Bible.

Moses, Adam, Noah, Solomon, David, Jesus, Lot, Joseph and Jacob are in the Koran and are all called prophets of Allah. The stories about these "prophets" are in much shortened versions and are much different than the ones in the Bible. The main gist of the stories of these "prophets" is that you must follow Allah's prophets and do what they say. Therefore, do what Mohammed says since he says that he is a prophet. Mohammed's only proof of being a prophet was to say that the Jews had prophets and he was their successor. His proof was assertion. Mohammed was a prophet

---

1   Mohammed said that there were seven versions of the Koran. An ancient Koran was found in Yemen that differs from the "official" version.

because he said he was. Muslims say that they have the true stories of the prophets and that Jews and Christians are wrong.

The Koran is divided into two parts—the early Koran written in Mecca and the later Koran written in Medina. The Meccan Koran has many Jewish stories and repeats that Mohammed is the prophet and everyone should do what he says. The later Medinan Koran is very political and condemns the Jews. It also contains many religious and legal rules. There are over 200 verses that contradict each other. This is part of the dual nature of the Koran. Islam has two contradictory things to say about any subject. Part of the duality is that both sides of the contradiction are true. Duality is the key to understanding Islam and it will be discussed in detail later.

A Word to Christians

There is a subtle trap for Christians in Islam. When many Christians hear that Islam's Koran came from Gabriel and that Islam has the same prophets as Christians and Jews, then Islam must be valid. This was Mohammed's biggest proof of his prophethood. But before anyone jumps to that conclusion, pay closer attention to the details.

Islam says that its Ibrahim is the same as Abraham, Musa is the same as Moses and that Isa is the same as Jesus. But when you read the Koran, you see that this is not true, if you know the Bible. The Koran does not confirm a single fact of the Bible, but instead spins it to serve Mohammed. Musa, Ibrahim and Isa of the Koran are not the Moses, Abraham, and Jesus of the Bible.

Allah and the Koran

Some English translations of the Koran use the word God instead of Allah. In an English speaking culture the word God is synonymous with the One-God, Jehovah/Yahweh, of the Jews and Christians. However, the meaning of both Allah and Jehovah/Yahweh is based upon their textual attributes. Allah is defined by the Koran. Jehovah/Yahweh is defined by the Old Testament. On a textual basis Jews, Muslims, and Christians do not worship the same God. As an example, red and blue are both colors, but red is not blue. Likewise, Allah and Jehovah/Yahweh are both a One-God, but they are not the same One-God. Allah is not Jehovah/Yahweh.

Arab Christians also use the word Allah. The word allah is derived from *ilah*, deity or god, and *al*, meaning *the*. So Allah means The-God. But the meaning of the name Allah of Arab Christians is taken from the Christian scriptures. The meaning of the name Allah of Islam comes from the

Koran. The Allah of Arab Christians is not the Allah of Islam. But for Arab Christians, Allah is the same as Jehovah.

Hence, Allah is the only acceptable term for the One-God of the Koran, not God.

Love and the Koran

While there are over 300 references in the Koran to Allah and fear, there are 49 references to love. Of these references, 39 are negative such as the 14 negative references to love of money, power, other gods and status.

Three verses command humanity to love Allah and 2 verses tell about how Allah loves a believer. There are 25 verses about how Allah does not love kafirs.

This leaves 5 verses about love. Of these 5, 3 are about loving kin or a Muslim brother. One verse commands a Muslim to give for the love of Allah. This leaves only one quasi-universal verse about love: give what you love to charity and even this is contaminated by dualism since Muslim charity only goes to other Muslims.

There is not a verse about either compassion or love of a kafir, but there are 14 verses that teach that a Muslim is not a friend of the kafir. There are 99 names for Allah and not one of them is love.

Islamic Hell is primarily political. Hell is mentioned 146 times in the Koran. Only 9 references are for moral failings—greed, lack of charity, or love of worldly success. The other 137 references to Hell involve eternal torture for disagreeing with Mohammed. Thus 94% of the references to Hell are as a political prison for dissenters.

HADITH

You have already read hadiths in the first lesson. A hadith is a single story about Mohammed. A complete book of hadiths is called a Hadith. [The naming is confusing, but that is the way it is. A lower case *h* is a single story, a capital *H* is a collection of stories.]

In the same way that Matthew, Mark, Luke and John tell the same story, there are many different Hadith collections. There are six collections of Hadith that are the most respected by all Muslims. There are other collections, but they are not as trusted. It is like there are four gospels—Matthew, Mark, Luke and John—but there are also the gospels of Thomas and Judas. Most Christians would not trust these books, but they are there. In the same way, most Muslims never use the less authoritative Hadith.

If this seems a little vague, it is. It also allows a Muslim to deny something he doesn't like. If you quote a hadith a Muslim does not like; he will say, "Oh, some of those hadiths are not so sure." All of the hadiths in these lessons are from the most trusted sources.

The most important Hadith is by a writer called Bukhari. He recorded about 6800 of these hadiths or Traditions. These lessons usually refer to him, but Abu Muslim and Abu Dawud [meaning David] are also quoted.

A hadith, or tradition, usually only a paragraph long, is an action, brief story, or conversation about or by Mohammed. The action can be as elementary as Mohammed's drinking a glass of water or tying his shoes.

The Hadith contains the *Sunna* (the ideal speech or action) of Mohammed, that is, his pronouncements. The actual words or deeds, then, that one should follow are the Sunna; the story that gave rise to the Sunna is the hadith.

All of the Hadith were written about 200 years after Mohammed's death. There are thousands of them and they form the most important sacred text of Islam. A Muslim's life is far more governed by the Hadith than the Koran.

The Rightly Guided Caliphs

There is one exception to the Sunna of Mohammed. There are four men who were Mohammed's companions—Abu Bakr, Ali, Umar and Uthman—who became caliphs (Islamic pope-kings) after Mohammed died. Their actions and words are also Sunna. So, what they did also is a perfect example of how a Muslim should live. The companions are similar to the Apostles in their authority.

SIRA

The life of Mohammed in Lesson 1 was taken from the Sira, Mohammed's biography. Hadith and Sira form the Sunna. Sira means a biography. The Sira has comparisons to Matthew, Mark, Luke and John. The most important biography is by Ibn Ishaq [meaning Isaac], *Sira Rasul Allah,* (The Way of the Apostle of Allah). It has been translated and is an 800 page book in fine print that is filled with Arabic terms. It is a complete biography of Mohammed. The Sira is a sacred text of Islam.

The language is very scholarly and difficult to comprehend in places. As a result, almost no one ever reads it, which is a shame because it is a great story in its own right. Mohammed starts off as an orphan and becomes the first king of Arabia.

The problem of the difficulty has been solved by condensing the text. Here is an example:

> Ishaq 774 The wealth taken from the beaten Jews of Khaybar and divided. A cavalry man got three shares, a foot soldier got one share. Mohammed appointed eighteen chiefs to divide the stolen wealth. Mohammed received his one-fifth before it was distributed.

The 774 is the margin note in the original text and serves the same function as chapter:verse in the Bible. The actual text from Ishaq 774:

> When the spoil of Khaybar was divided, al-Shaqq and Nata fell to the Muslims while al-Katiba was divided into five sections: God's fifth; the prophet's share (T. fifth); the share of kindred, orphans, the poor (T. and wayfarers); maintenance of the prophet's wives; and maintenance of the men who acted as intermediaries in the peace negotiations with the men of Fadak. To Muhayyisa, who was one of these men, the apostle gave thirty loads of barley and thirty loads of dates. Khaybar was apportioned among the men of al-Hudaybiya without regard to whether they were present at Khaybar or not. Only Jabir b. 'Abdullah b. 'Amr b. Haram was absent and the apostle gave him the same share as the others. Its two wadis, alSurayr and Khass, formed the territory into which Khaybar was divided. Nata and al-Shaqq formed 18 shares of which Nata formed 5 and al-Shaqq 13. These two places were divided into 1,800 shares.
>
> The number of the companions among whom Khaybar was divided was 1,800 with shares for horse and foot; 1,400 men and 200 horses; every horse got two shares and his rider one; every footman got one share. There was a chief over every allotment for every 100 men, i.e. 18 blocks of shares.

RELIGIOUS AND POLITICAL ISLAM

Islam is a civilization with a political system, a culture, and a religion. The religion of Islam is what a Muslim does to go to Paradise and avoid Hell. Political Islam determines the treatment of unbelievers and the governance of Muslims. The internal politics of Islam are not of interest here.

The Five Pillars of Islam are:

1. Charity to other Muslims
2. Prayer to Allah
3. Fasting during the month of Ramadan
4. Pilgrimage to Mecca

5.   Declaring that Mohammed is the prophet of the only god, Allah

The religion of Islam is important to Muslims, but the politics affect every non-Muslim.

Islam has a complete legal code, the Sharia. The foundation of Islam's legal and political system is clearly laid out in three texts—the Koran, the Sira, and the Hadith—the Islamic Trilogy. Every book of the Trilogy is both religious and political. More than half of the Koran focuses on the unbelievers. About three-quarters of the Sira (life of Mohammed) is political. The Hadith is filled with political statements and examples. Islam is a fully developed political system. The fundamental principle of Islam is that its politics are sacred, perfect, eternal, and universal. All other political systems are man-made and must be replaced by Islamic law.

Islam's success comes primarily from its politics. In Mohammed's first thirteen years as a spiritual leader, he converted 150 people to his religion. When he became a political leader and warrior, Islam exploded, and Mohammed became king of Arabia in ten years.

The Trilogy defines Islam. The kafir must submit to Islam. This is a political statement because it is the nature of Islam that it must control the public space—law, custom, the courts, art, the media and the schools. The power of Islam is its politics, not in the religion. He failed as a prophet and succeeded as a politician and war lord.

The Trilogy is very political. Over half of the Koran is about what to do to and about the kafir. About 75% of the Sira is about politics and jihad. About a quarter of the Hadith is about jihad and what to do about the kafir. In short, Islam is both a religion and a political system.

One of the best ways to see how political Islam is to simply count the amount of words devoted to the kafir and politics in each text.

Koran	Sira	Hadith
61%	75%	20%

Amount of Each Text Devoted to Politics and Kafirs

What Islam does to other religions is political, not religious. The best mental image of Islam is communism with a god. The religion of Islam is its invisibility cloak for its real strength—politics.

KAFIR

Most of the Koran is about the non-Muslims. It has special names for all the different types of people who don't believe Mohammed.

One of these names that the Koran uses is *kafir*. This word is usually translated as unbeliever, but this is wrong.

One of the greatest failings of non-Muslims is the use of language to describe Islam. The words that non-Muslims use never show any real understanding of Islam. Take for example, the word unbeliever. Unbeliever is logically correct, but the problem is that it does not go far enough. Unbeliever is emotionally neutral. Kafir is negatively charged to a degree that has no equal in English. We do not have a word in the English language that is as bigoted as kafir. And the worst part is that, for a Muslim, it is not that he thinks you are a kafir, but Allah says that you are a kafir.

The Koran defines the kafir and says that the kafir is hated and despised by Allah. A kafir can be mocked, tortured, punished, killed, beheaded, confused, plotted against, terrorized, destroyed, deceived, caused pain, cut down, cheated, insulted, subjugated, made war on, and humiliated.

A kafir is ignorant, blind, arrogant, evil, a liar, disgraced, a partner of Satan, doomed, detested, unclean and cursed. So says the Koran.

A Muslim is not the friend of the kafir. In all of the Trilogy, there is not one neutral description of the kafir. Each and every sentence that uses kafir is negative, antagonistic, bigoted and hateful.

Kafir is a unique word. Kafir is the sacred, absolute, complete, final and universal truth of Allah about all non-Muslims. Kafir is the real word— unbeliever is a pretend word that is a denial of the doctrine of Islam.

Christians and Jews are not only kafirs but infidels as well. Christians are called infidels because they are not "faithful" to the "real" word of Allah, the Koran.

This work will not use the word unbeliever, and as a Christian you should never use any word except kafir. It shows that you understand the real Islam and that you reject the media's cotton-candy approach to Islam. Be proud to be a kafir.

QUESTIONS

Some people say that the Koran is Islam's Bible. What is actually the Islamic Bible? Why?

Why do you think that Uthman burned all the orginal source texts after compiling the Koran?

What are the two Korans?

Why is it more important to call yourself a kafir than an unbeliever?

Some Christian preachers say that Muslims worship the same god as the Christians. What do you think? Why do you think they say that?

What is the difference between religious Islam and political Islam?

What is the difference between the Hadith and a hadith?

What is the proper relationship between Allah and Muslims?

What are the Five Pillars of Islam?

Christians like to say that Jesus loves you. Does Allah love you?

What does it say to the world and a Muslim when you use the word kafir for yourself?

JIHAD

Lesson 3

SUMMARY

- Jihad was developed by Mohammed in Medina, where he turned to politics and war.
- Jihad started as raids on the Meccans. It then progressed into open war. The nature of the Koran changed from religious to political. It became a basis for war against all kafirs.
- Mohammed won his first battle at Badr and then lost his next battle. After that, he never lost. He entered Mecca by conquest ten years after he left.
- The Koran says all Muslims are to take part in jihad, to the limit of their abilities. The Hadith is filled with the rules of jihad.

Jihad was a unique invention by Mohammed. Islam was a failure until it started practicing jihad. The actual meaning of jihad is not war, but struggle. Harb is the Arabic word for war.

Another misunderstanding about jihad is that it strictly killing. Not so. Jihad is all of the struggle against the kafirs. Writing a letter to the editor about peaceful Islam is jihad. Claiming that the Declaration of Independence is based upon Islamic principles (yes, they do that) is jihad. Giving money to Islamic charities for jihadists is jihad. When a Muslim marries a Christian girl that is jihad, because all of the children must be raised as Muslims. All struggle against the kafirs is jihad.

Jihad is done with the tongue, the pen, money and the sword.

A THUMBNAIL SKETCH OF MOHAMMED'S JIHAD

Jihad did not begin until Mohammed was in Medina for a year. After a year in Medina, the Muslims were poor. The Meccan trade caravans regularly passed near Medina. Here was a way to get money and take revenge on those who had run Mohammed out of Mecca.

Ishaq 425 Islam drew first blood against the Quraysh of Mecca. They attacked the unarmed caravan. Amr, the first man to be killed by jihad, was shot by an arrow. One man escaped, and they captured two others. The

Muslims took the enemies' camels with their goods and headed back to Medina and Mohammed. On the way they talked about how Mohammed would get one fifth of the stolen goods.

The Meccans got a small army and went to Medina to fight Mohammed. The Meccans and the Muslims met at the well of Badr. It was the morning of the battle:

Ishaq 440 As Mohammed saw the Quraysh march into the small valley, he said, "O Allah, here come the Quraysh, in their vanity and pride, contending with You and calling me a liar. O Allah, give me the help You promised. Destroy them this morning!"

Ishaq 445 It was time for the two armies to close ranks and move forward. Mohammed had said his warriors were not to start until he gave the order. Now he took a handful of pebbles and threw them at the Quraysh and said, "Curse those faces." The Muslims advanced. The battle had begun.

The Muslims were outnumbered but won the battle.

Ishaq 446 As the battle was ending and the prisoners were being rounded up, Mohammed saw a look of disgust on Saed's face. He said, "You seem to dislike what you see." Saed replied, "Yes, by Allah, this is our first defeat of the kafirs and we should slaughter them all to the last man."

> Koran 8:67 *A prophet should not take prisoners of war until he has fought and slaughtered in the land. You desire the bounty of the world, but Allah desires the bounty for you of the world to come. Allah is mighty and wise.*

Ishaq 451 As the battle wound down, Mohammed issued orders for the fighters to be on the lookout for Abu Jahl, the enemy of Allah, among the slain. He was found still fighting in a thicket. When a Muslim fighter got to within striking distance of Abu Jahl, the Muslim made for him and cut off his lower leg and sent it flying. Another Muslim passed as Abu Jahl lay dying and put his foot on his neck. The Muslim said, "Has Allah put you to shame, enemy of Allah?" Abu Jahl gasped, "How has He shamed me? Am I any more remarkable than any other you have killed?" The Muslim cut off his head.

Ishaq 452 He took the head back to Mohammed and said, "Here is the head of the enemy of Allah," and threw it at Mohammed's feet. The prophet said, "Praise be to Allah."

Ishaq 454 The bodies of the Quraysh were thrown into a well. The Apostle of Allah leaned over the well and shouted at the bodies, "O people of the well, have you found what Allah promised to be true?" The Muslims were puzzled by his question. "Are you speaking to dead people?" they asked. Mohammed explained that the dead could understand him.

The Koran is very clear. The Muslims won due the help of angels.

Ishaq 477 The Muslims had not fought by themselves. Allah had sent a thousand angels to help kill those who worshiped in the ancient ways and rituals. To resist Mohammed was a death sentence from Allah.

> Koran 8:12 *Then your Lord spoke to His angels and said, "I will be with you. Give strength to the believers. I will send terror into the kafirs' hearts, cut off their heads and even the tips of their fingers!" This was because they opposed Allah and His messenger. Ones who oppose Allah and His messenger will be severely punished by Allah. We said, "This is for you! Taste it and know that the kafirs will receive the torment of the Fire."*

Ishaq 484 Mohammed was now a political force unlike any ever seen in history. The fusion of religion and politics with a universal mandate created a permanent force. The treasure of war, the spoils, will provide the wealth of Islam. The awe of Mohammed is the fear of Allah.

> Bukhari 1,7,331 *The Prophet said, "I have been given five things which were not given to anyone else before me.*
>
> 1. *Allah made me victorious by awe, by His frightening my enemies for a distance of one month's journey.*
>
> 2. *The earth has been made for me and for my followers a place for praying and to perform my rituals; therefore, anyone of my followers can pray whenever the time of a prayer is due.*
>
> 3. *The spoils of war have been made lawful for me yet they were not lawful for anyone else before me.*
>
> 4. *I have been given the right of intercession on the Day of Resurrection.*
>
> 5. *Every Prophet was sent to his nation but only I have been sent to all mankind."*

After a year in Medina there were 250 to 300 Muslims, up from the 150 in Mecca. After the Battle of Badr, a new Islam emerged. Mohammed rode out of Medina as a politician and a general. Islam became an armed political force with a religious motivation, jihad. After Badr, the Muslims were prosperous and they gained in power.

The next large battle was when the Meccans returned the next year and fought Islam at Uhud. The Muslims lost and Mohammed was wounded. This caused a crisis in Islam. Allah had sent a thousand angels to help defeat the kafirs at Badr. What happened?

Ishaq 595 The reason for the Muslim loss was that the archers did not hold their ground. When they saw that the Meccans were cut off from their camp, they ran to get the treasure of war. Greed caused them to dis-obey Mohammed. They were told they should always obey Mohammed; he spoke for the Lord of all.

Ishaq 597 The reason Allah let the Meccans win was to test the Muslims. Now they truly knew themselves. Were they fair-weather friends of Mo-hammed, or could they see their faults? If they obeyed Mohammed, then they could become true Muslims. A true Muslim never lost his morale, never fell into despair.

> Koran 3:139 *Therefore, do not lose heart or despair; if you are a true be-liever, you will be victorious.*

Ishaq 599 Jihad wasn't over. Soon Islam would bring terror to the kafirs. After death they would burn in Hell. Their destruction would come be-cause they did not believe in the religion of Islam.

> Koran 3:151 *We will strike terror into the hearts of the kafirs because they worship others besides Allah, which He gave them no permission to do. Their home will be the Fire, a terrible resting place for the evildoers.*

The next large conflict was called the Battle of the Ditch. The Meccans returned to Medina and were held off by the defensive measure of a trench or ditch. This was the first time this defensive measure had been used in Arabia. Militarily, the battle was a draw. Politically, it was a victory for Is-lam, because the Meccans had tried to crush Islam and failed.

Between all the big battles, Islam waged jihad against the nearest tribes. The jihadists took caravans, enslaved kafirs and killed those who resisted political Islam. For nine years Mohammed sent out fighters on the average of every six weeks.

Mohammed took a large number of people to go on a pilgrimage to Mecca. [Arabs had been going to Mecca for religious pilgrimages for many years before Mohammed. Mohammed incorporated most of the pagan practices into Islam.] The Meccans met him outside and forbade the Mus-lims entrance to Mecca. Mohammed signed a treaty with the Meccans. This treaty was a political victory for Mohammed.

Ishaq 750 Mohammed regarded the treaty with the Meccans as an oath to Allah and a victory for Islam. The government of Mecca had dealt with Mohammed as an independent political power. Many more Arabs were attracted to the religion of Islam now that it was rich and powerful.

The treaty at al Hudaybiya established Islam's attitudes about treaties to this day. Islam makes a treaty, if and only if, it is in a losing position. The treaty is good only as long as it is weak. When Islam is strong, jihad will start again.

Koran 47:33 *Believers! Obey Allah and the messenger, and do not let your effort be in vain. Those who do not believe and who prevent others from following Allah's path and then die as kafirs will not receive Allah's forgiveness. Therefore, do not be weak and offer the kafirs peace when you have the upper hand, for Allah is with you and will not begrudge you the reward of your deeds.*

About a year later, Mohammed found a reason to break the treaty of Hudaybiya. He had been making raids against kafir tribes, gaining wealth and converts. Islam was stronger than when he made the treaty. It was time and he marched against Mecca with an army of 10,000.

Mecca surrendered without a fight. Islam triumphed.

Ishaq 819 Mohammed had told his commanders to kill only those who resisted; otherwise they were not to bother anyone except for those who had spoken against Mohammed. He then issued death warrants for all of those in Mecca who had resisted Islam.

Ishaq 821 Mohammed went to the Kabah and rode around it seven times. Each time he went past the Black Stone[1], he touched it with his stick. Then he called for the key to the Kabah and entered. Inside was a carved wooden dove that he picked up and broke and threw out the door. There were also ritual objects and art of the various Arab faiths. Mohammed had them all burned and destroyed.

Mohammed's second order of business after assuming power was to destroy all religious art. The perfect pattern of Islam, aesthetics, and art was established.

Mohammed fought two more large battles before his death.

JIHAD

The political system of jihad is based upon ethical dualism. Jihad is defined in the Trilogy. In the Sira, jihad is war against the kafir. There is a second kind of jihad found in the Hadith called the greater jihad, which is inner, spiritual struggle. However, by actual count, only 3% of the jihad hadiths in Bukhari are about inner, spiritual struggle; 97% of the hadith refer to war against the kafir. In the Koran, jihad is called "struggle in the cause of Allah." And 100% of the "struggle in the cause of Allah" is devoted to killing, enslaving and berating the kafir until the kafir submits to Islam.

---

1 The Kabah in Mecca is made of stone. In one corner there is a black stone that is held sacred to Islam because of Mohammed.

Jihad is a political method with political goals. The goal of jihad is to make the kafir submit to Islam. The only reason that Mohammed ever attacked anyone was purely based upon the fact that they had not submitted to his god, Allah.

Muslims kill other Muslims, but that is never jihad. Jihad is reserved for the kafir. The subtext of kafir is that the kafir has offended Allah by rejecting Him. Hence, all jihad is defensive. Jihad is always caused by the offense of unbelief. Jihad is pure political dualism.

A NOTE

A careful study of the Koran shows its sources are the Old Testament, Jewish folk tales, unorthodox Christianity, and pagan Arabic religions. There is only one thing that Mohammed actually created that was new—jihad. It was jihad that made Islam powerful under Mohammed and it was jihad that created the Islamic empire. It is jihad today that makes Islam powerful.

The Sira is a strategic manual of jihad. The Hadith is a tactical manual of jihad.

JIHAD AND THE HADITH

To be a real Muslim, one must aspire to be a jihadist.

> Muslim 020,4696 *Mohammed: "The man who dies without participating in jihad, who never desired to wage holy war, dies the death of a hypocrite."*

Here is Allah's contract with all Islam: to die in jihad is the sure way to go to Paradise. If the jihadist does not die, then he can keep what wealth he takes with violence from the enemy, the non-Muslim.

> Bukhari 4,52,46 *Mohammed: "A Muslim holy warrior, fighting for Allah's cause is like a person who does nothing but fast and pray. Allah promises that anyone killed while fighting for His cause will be admitted without question into Paradise. If such a holy warrior survives the battles, he can return home with the captured property and possessions of the defeated."*

A Muslim should support jihadists in every way. This includes financing the fighters and supporting their families. Today this is done through Islamic charities.

> Bukhari 4,52,96 *Mohammed: "Anyone who arms a jihadist is rewarded just as a fighter would be; anyone who gives proper care*

to a holy warrior's dependents is rewarded just as a fighter would be."

Allah rewards those who give to jihad and curses those who do not.

Bukhari 2,24,522 *Mohammed: "Two angels descend from Paradise each day. One says, 'O, Allah! Reward those who contribute to jihad,' and the other says, 'O, Allah! Kill those who refuse to support jihad.'"*

Muslim 020,4649 *Mohammed: "Except debt, all sins of a martyr are forgiven."*

Mohammed often used money to influence others about Islam and keep new converts.

Bukhari 4,53,374 *Mohammed: "I give money to the Quraysh to tempt them into remaining true to Islam, because they are new to the faith and their lives of ignorance are a short distance away."*

To die in jihad is the best life.

Bukhari 5,59,377 *During the battle of Uhud, a man asked Mohammed, "Where will I go if I am killed in battle?" Mohammed said, "Paradise." The man then threw away the meal that he was carrying, joined the battle, and fought until he was killed.*

Forcing themselves on the female captives of jihad was standard practice for Mohammed and his companions. Attractive female captives became slaves used for pleasure, and Mohammed had his choice of the most attractive new slaves. This is the ideal pattern of Islam.

Bukhari 3,34,431 *One of the captives was a beautiful Jewess, Safiya. Dihya had her first, but she was given to Mohammed next.*

Mohammed accepted jihadists forcing themselves on kafir women.

Bukhari 3,34,432 *While sitting with Mohammed, I [Abu Said Al-Khudri] asked, "Mohammed, sometimes we receive female slaves as our share of the spoils. Naturally, we are concerned about their retaining their value [the slaves of pleasure were worth less money if they were pregnant when sold]. How do you feel about withdrawal?" Mohammed asked, "Do you do that? It is better not to do that. It is Allah's will whether or not a child is born."*

The Jews were date farmers. One of the tactics of jihad is to attack economic assets [This was a goal of September 11, 2001 attack].

Bukhari 3,39,519 *Mohammed destroyed the date orchards of the Jews and Hassan wrote this poetic verse: "The chiefs of Bani LuAi enjoyed watching the Jew's trees consumed by fire."*

The poetry of this hadith is the most elegant expression of jihad.

Bukhari 4,52,73 *Mohammed: "Be aware that Paradise lies under the shadow of swords."*

QUESTIONS

What are the different kinds of jihad?

What is the difference between war (harb) and jihad?

Why is the battle of Badr one of the most important battles of all history?

What were the five things that Mohammed was given? Which of them are political? Religious?

Today a jihadist is never discouraged when they fail. What battle of Mohammed do they draw lessons from?

If Islam offers to make a treaty, what does that mean about them? What will happen later?

Muslims say the the real jihad is the inner struggle. What does the life of Mohammed teach us about jihad?

What is every Muslim's obligation to jihad?

Examine the 9/11 attack on the World Trade Towers. How were the attacks pure jihad?

THE JEWS

Lesson 4

SUMMARY

- At first Mohammed used the Old Testament to "prove" that he was a real prophet, just like Moses, Noah and the others. When Mohammed moved to Medina, which had many Jews, trouble with the Jews started. The Jews said that Mohammed was not a prophet in the line of the Jews.
- After arguing with the Jews, Mohammed turned his jihad on them. He systematically annihilated all three tribes of Jews. He took all of the wealth of the first two tribes and then he exiled them. He killed all of the men of the third tribe and sold the women and children into slavery.

Mohammed made both the Jews and Judaism submit to Islam. There are no Jews or Christians in Arabia today, not one, because of Mohammed. The war in Israel today is also because of Mohammed.

Islam's relationship with the Jews is dualistic. At first the Koran and Mohammed use the Jews as proof of Mohammed's mission. The whole thrust of the Meccan Koran is that Mohammed is a new and better Jewish prophet. The Koran retells the stories of Adam, Moses, Noah, Lot, Abraham, David, Solomon and Joseph. In every case they have been reworked to "prove" that all the world should listen to the final prophet, Mohammed, and do just what he says.

If you know the story of Mohammed in Mecca, the Jewish stories are mostly Mohammed's situation in disguise. The story of Noah is transparently the story of Mohammed. The words that Noah says are identical to Mohammed's words. What the people say to Noah are the same as what the Meccans say to Mohammed. Here is a typical Noah story from the Koran:

> Koran 23:23 *It can not be disputed that We sent Noah to his people, and he said, "Oh, My people! Serve Allah. You have no other god but Him. Will you not fear Him?" But the chiefs of the kafirs said, "He is a mere mortal, just like yourselves, who wishes to make himself superior to you. If Allah wished to send a message, then He would have sent angels. We have never*

28

heard of such a thing from our ancestors." Others said, "He is only a mad-man; be patient with him for a while."

23:26 *Noah said, "My Lord, help me. They accuse me of lying." So We inspired him with Our revelation: "Make an ark under Our eye and guidance. When We command and when the oceans overflow, load onto the ark pairs of every creature and your followers except those who have already been damned. Do not plead with Me on behalf of the wicked be-cause they will be drowned.*

Again, the words of the kafirs are identical to what the Meccans said. So Mohammed was the new Noah. This is the essence of the Koran of Mecca; Mohammed is the last of Allah's prophets. The god of Noah and the rest of the Jewish prophets was actually Allah and Noah was a Muslim.

THE JEWS

When Mohammed came to Medina there were three tribes of Jews and two tribes of Arabs. Almost none of the Jews had Hebrew names. They were Arabs to some degree. At the same time many of the Arabs' reli-gious practices had elements of Judaism. The Jews were farmers and tradesmen and lived in their own fortified quarters. In general they were better educated and more prosperous than the Arabs.

Before Mohammed arrived, there had been bad blood and killing among the tribes. The last battle had been fought by the two Arab tribes, but each of the Jewish tribes had joined the battle with its particular Arab allies. In addition to that tension between the two Arab tribes, there was a tension between the Jews and the Arabs. The division of the Jews and fighting on different sides was condemned by Mohammed. The Torah preached that the Jews should be unified, and they failed in this.

All of these quarrelsome tribal relationships were one reason that Mo-hammed was invited to Medina. But the result was further polarization, not unity. The new split was between Islam and those Arabs and their Jewish partners who resisted Islam.

The Koran repeats the many favors that Allah has done for the Jews—they were the chosen people, delivered from slavery under the pharaoh, given the sacred Torah, and yet all they have ever done was to sin. They have been forgiven many times by Allah, and still, they are as hard as rocks and refuse to believe Mohammed.

Koran 2:174 *Those [the Jews] who conceal any part of the Scriptures which Allah has revealed in order to gain a small profit shall ingest nothing but Fire in their stomachs. Allah will not speak to them on the Day of Resur-rection, and they will pay a painful penalty.*

The Koran says that the Jews' sins were so great that Allah had changed them into apes. Still they would not learn and refused to admit that Mohammed was their prophet. They knew full well the truth and hid and confused others. Even when they said to Mohammed they believed, they concealed their resistance.

> Koran 7:165 *When they disregarded the warnings that had been given to them [not to work on the Sabbath], We rescued those who had forbidden wrongdoing, and We punished the wrongdoers for their transgressions. But when they persisted in what they had been forbidden, We said to them, "Be as apes, despised and loathed." [The Jews were changed into apes.]*

To this day, Muslims refer to Jews as apes, monkeys or pigs. There is a hadith in which Mohammed says that Jews are rats as well. Christians are referred to as pigs and dogs.

Since Islam is the successor to Judaism, Allah was the successor to Jehovah. It was actually Allah who had been the deity of the Jews and the Jews had deliberately hidden this fact by corrupted scriptures. For this the Jews would be cursed.

> Koran 2:159 *Those who conceal the clear signs and guidance [Mohammed said that the Jews corrupted the Scriptures that predicted his prophecy] that We have sent down after We have made them clear in the Scriptures for mankind, will receive Allah's curse and the curse of those who damn them.*

Ishaq 545 There were three tribes of Jews in Medina. The Beni Qaynuqa were goldsmiths and lived in a stronghold in their quarters. It is said by Mohammed that they broke the treaty that had been signed when Mohammed came to Medina. [How they did this is unclear from the text.]

Ishaq 545 Mohammed assembled the Jews in their market and said: "Oh Jews, be careful that Allah does not bring vengeance upon you like what happened to the Quraysh. Become Muslims. You know that I am the prophet that was sent you. You will find that in your scriptures."

Ishaq 546 Some time later Mohammed besieged the Jews in the their quarters. None of the other two Jewish tribes came to their support. Finally the Jews surrendered and expected to be slaughtered after their capture.

Mohammed exiled the Jews and took all of their wealth and goods.

THE ASSASSINATION OF AL ASHRAF, THE JEW

Ishaq 548 When Al Ashraf, a Jew of Medina, heard that two of his friends had been killed at the battle of Badr, he said that the grave was a better place than the earth with Mohammed. So the "enemy of Allah" composed some poems bewailing the loss of his friends and attacking Islam.

Ishaq 551 When Mohammed heard of Al Ashraf's criticism of his politics, he said, "Who will rid me of Al Ashraf?" A Muslim said, "I will kill him for you." Days later Mohammed found out that his assassin was not doing anything, including eating or drinking. Mohammed summoned him and asked what was going on. The man replied that he had taken on a task that was too difficult for him to do. Mohammed said that it was a duty which he should try to do. The assassin said, "Oh Apostle of Allah, I will have to tell a lie." The Prophet said, "Say what you like, you are free in the matter."

Ishaq 552 By the use of lies three Muslims were able to kill Al Ashraf. When they returned to Mohammed, he was praying. They told him that they had killed the enemy of Allah. Their attack terrorized all the Jews. There was no Jew in Medina who was not afraid.

This story is very important. It is the sacred example of lying and deceiving the kafirs. Assassination is important in jihad. Artists and intellectuals can be killed if they offend Islam. Artists and intellectuals fear Islam, but they keep silent about their fear. When the newspapers would not publish the Danish Mohammed cartoons, they gave all manner of "sensitivity" excuses. But the reason was pure fear. Notice how the media is quick to criticize Christianity, but not Islam. Fear. Pure fear.

KILL ANY JEW THAT FALLS INTO YOUR POWER

Ishaq 554 The Apostle of Allah said, "Kill any Jew who falls into your power." Hearing this Muhayyisa fell upon a Jewish merchant who was a business associate and killed him. His brother was not a Muslim and asked him how he could kill a man who had been his friend and partner in many business deals. The Muslim said that if Mohammed had asked him to kill his brother he would have done it immediately. His brother said, "You mean that if Mohammed said to cut off my head you would do it?" "Yes," was the reply. The older brother then said, "By Allah, any religion which brings you to this is marvelous." And he decided then and there to become a Muslim.

It came time for Mohammed to destroy the second Jewish tribe of Medina.

Ishaq 652 It had been four years since Mohammed came to Medina. Mohammed went to one of the two remaining Jewish tribes to ask for blood money for the two men his fighter had killed. At first they said yes, but as they talked about it they decided that this would be a good time to kill Mohammed. Here he was in their quarter of Medina sitting on a wall near a roof. Why not send a man up and drop a rock on this man who had been such a sorrow to them? Mohammed got word of the plot and left.

Ishaq 653 This was as good a reason as any to deal with the Jews. The same Jews who insisted that he was not the prophet. He raised his army and went off to put their fortresses under siege. These Jews were farmers and they grew the finest dates in all of Arabia. So Mohammed cut and burned their date palms as they watched. They called out, "You have prohibited wanton destruction and blamed those who do that. Now you do what you forbid."

Ishaq 653 Now the other Jewish tribe had assured them that they would come to their defense. But no Jew would stand with another Jew against Islam. With no help from their brothers, the besieged Jews cut a deal with the apostle of Allah. Spare their lives and let them go with what they could carry on their camels, except for their armor.

THE DESTRUCTION OF THE LAST TRIBE OF JEWS IN MEDINA

Ishaq 684 That same day the angel Gabriel came to Mohammed at noon. He asked if Mohammed was through fighting? Gabriel said that he and the angels were going to attack the last Jewish tribe in Medina. Gabriel said, "Allah commands you to go to the Jews. I am headed there now to shake their stronghold."

Ishaq 684 So Mohammed called upon his troops and they headed to the forts of the Jews. Now the Jews of Medina lived in forts that were on the outskirts of Medina. Mohammed rode up to the forts and called out, "You brothers of apes, has Allah disgraced you and brought His vengeance upon you?"

Ishaq 685-689 Mohammed put the Jews under siege for twenty-five days. Finally, the Jews offered to submit their fate to a Muslim, Saed, with whom they had had been an ally in the past. His judgment was simple. Kill all the men. Take their property and take the women and children as captives. Mohammed said, "You have given the judgment of Allah."

Ishaq 690 The captives were taken into Medina. They dug trenches in the market place of Medina. It was a long day, but 800 Jews met their death that day. Mohammed and his twelve year old wife sat and watched the entire day and into the night. The Apostle of Allah had every male Jew killed by beheading.

Ishaq 693 Mohammed took the property, wives and children of the Jews, and divided it up amongst the Muslims. Mohammed took his one fifth of the slaves and sent a Muslim with the female Jewish slaves to a nearby city where the women were sold for pleasure. Mohammed invested the money from the sale of the female slaves for horses and weapons.

Ishaq 693 There was one last piece of spoils for Mohammed. The most beautiful Jewess was his slave for pleasure.

THE KILLING OF THE JEW, SALLAM

Ishaq 714-6 A Jew named Sallam helped to plan and organize the confederation of the tribes that attacked Mohammed in the Battle of the Trench. Mohammed sent five Muslim men to assassinate Sallam. When the men had done their work, they returned to Mohammed and fell to arguing as to who actually killed Sallam. Mohammed demanded to see their swords. He examined them one by one and then pointed to the sword that had been the killing weapon. It had food on it still from the thrust to the stomach.

But after annihilating the Jews of Medina, Mohammed was not through. He had two more tasks—dhimmitude and banishment.

ISLAMIC JEW HATRED

The Koran written in Medina is very hateful towards the Jews. Based upon word count, 10.6% of the material is anti-Semitic. To put this in perspective, if you read Hitler's *Mein Kampf,* and make a word count, it is 6.8% anti-Semitic. So the Medinan Koran is more anti-Jew than *Mein Kampf.*

As an aside, mein kamph means "my struggle" and jihad means "struggle" as well.

Today, anti-Semitism is on the rise in Europe, fueled by Islam and the Left.

QUESTIONS

How did Mohammed use the Jews to prove he was a prophet?

Notice that both Mohammed and the Koran use insults. What does that imply that Muslims will do?

Mohammed assassinated his enemies. What threats and killings do you know of by jihadists?

What could make you an enemy of Islam?

In the killing of Al Ashraf, the Muslims told a lie to advance Islam. What conclusions can we draw from this?

What does it mean to say that lies and deceit are Sunna?

How do Islamic ethics differ from Christian ethics?

CHRISTIANS

Lesson 5

SUMMARY

- Koranic doctrine: Jesus was a Muslim prophet who could do miracles through Allah. Jesus was born of Mary by virgin birth. He was not crucified but taken up to Paradise. The Christian Trinity is God, Jesus and Mary. The Gospels are corrupt and in error.

- The Koran says: The only true Christians are those who accept Mohammed as the prophet of Christianity. Christians must accept the political domination of Islam.

Christians, like the Jews, were called the People of the Book in the Koran. Although there were only a few Jews in Mecca, there were several Christians. When Mohammed returned to the house after his first vision of what he said was an angel, Khadija, Mohammed's first wife, sent for her cousin who was a Christian. The Christian said that Mohammed had been in communication with Gabriel. How he knew this from the evidence is not clear to us today.

After that, Mohammed had little to say about Christianity in Mecca.

Ishaq 404 While some Christians were in Medina, they argued religion with Mohammed. They held forth with the doctrine of the Trinity and the divinity of Christ. Mohammed later laid out the Islamic view of the Christian doctrine. The Koran tells in detail its version of Jesus, who was just another of Allah's prophets, and that the Trinity of the Christians was Allah, Jesus and Mary.

JESUS

Ishaq 406 No one has power except through Allah. Allah gave the prophet Jesus the power of raising the dead, healing the sick, making birds of clay and having them fly away. Allah gave Jesus these signs as a mark of his being a prophet. But Allah did not give the powers of appointing kings, the ability to change night to day. These lacks of power show that Jesus was a man, not part of a Trinity. If he were part of God, then all powers would

35

have been in his command. Then he would not have to have been under the dominion of kings.

Ishaq 407-8 Christ spoke in the cradle and then spoke to men as a grown man. Speaking from the cradle is a sign of his being a prophet. Christ's prophethood was confirmed by making clay birds fly[1]. By Allah, Christ healed the blind, the lepers, and raised the dead.

Ishaq 408 Christ only comes through Allah. Christ's signs of being a prophet come only from Allah. Jesus enjoins others to worship Allah, not him. But people refused to hear him, the Disciples came forth to help him with his mission. The Disciples were servants of Allah and were Muslims just like Christ.

Islam teaches that Christ was a prophet born of virgin birth.

> Koran 3:44 *This is one of the secret revelations revealed to you, Mohammed. You were not there when they cast their lots to see who would have guardianship of Mary, nor were you there when they argued about her. And remember when the angels said to Mary, "Allah brings you good news of His Word. His name will be Messiah, Jesus, Son of Mary, worthy of honor in this world and the world to come, one who is near to Allah. He will speak to the people when in the cradle and as a man. He will live a righteous life." She said, "My Lord! How can I have a son when no man has ever touched me?" He said, "It will be so. Allah creates what He will, and when He decrees a plan, all He must do is say, 'Be' and it is!" Allah will teach him the Scriptures and Wisdom, the Law, and the Gospel. He will be sent out as a messenger to the Children of Israel saying, "I have come to you with a sign from your Lord. I will make a figure of a bird out of clay and then, by Allah's will, I will breathe life into it. By Allah's permission I cause the blind to see, heal the lepers, and bring the dead back to life. I will tell you what you should eat and what you should store up in your houses. This will be a sign for those who truly believe. I have come to fulfill the Law which came before me and to give you permission to do certain things which were once unlawful. I come to you with a sign from your Lord, so fear Allah and obey me. Allah is my Lord and yours, so worship Him. That is the right path."*

> Koran 3:52 *When Jesus saw that they did not believe, he said, "Who will be my helpers for Allah?" The disciples replied, "We will be Allah's helpers! We believe in Allah and witness our submission to Him. Lord! We believe in what you have revealed and we follow Your messenger; therefore, record us as Your witnesses."*

---

1   The story about the clay birds is found in a heretical Christian church in Syria and Egypt. The Koran's odd stories about Christians and Jews are found in heretical texts.

Ishaq 409 Christ was not crucified. When the Jews plotted against Christ, they found Allah to be the best plotter. Allah took Jesus up directly to him and will refute those who say he was crucified and was resurrected. On the final day, the Day of Resurrection, those who follow Christ but do not believe in his divinity will be blessed. Those who insist that Christ is God, part of the Trinity, and reject true faith will be punished in Hell.

> Koran 3:54 *So the Jews plotted and Allah plotted, but Allah is the best of plotters. And Allah said, "Jesus! I am going to end your life on earth and lift you up to Me. [Jesus did not die on the cross. He was taken to Allah. He will return to kill the anti-Christ and then die a natural death.] I will send the kafirs away from you and lift up those who believe above all others until the Day of Resurrection. Then all will return to Me and I will judge their disputes. As for the kafirs, they will be punished with excruciating agony in this world and the world to come. They will have no one to help them. As for the believers who do good works, He will fully reward them. Allah does not love those who do wrong. These signs and this wise warning We bring to you."*
>
> 3:59 *Truly, Jesus is like Adam [neither had a father] in Allah's sight. He created him from the dust and said to him, "Be!" and he was.*

The Trinity of the Koran is Allah, Jesus and Mary. Where did Mohammed get this idea? There was a form of Christianity in Syria unlike any found today. Mohammed routinely went on trading trips to the area that taught this doctrine.

> Koran 4:171 *People of the Book [Christians]! Do not overstep the boundaries of your religion and speak only what is true about Allah. The Messiah, Jesus, the son of Mary, is only Allah's messenger and his Word which he sent into Mary was a spirit from Him. Therefore, believe in Allah and His messengers and do not say, "Trinity." Hold back and it will be better for you. Allah is only one god. Far be it from Allah to have a son! All in the heavens and earth are His. Allah is the sufficient as a protector. The Messiah does not condescend to be Allah's servant, nor do His favored angels. Those who disdain service to Him, and are filled with arrogance, Allah will gather them all together before Him.*

Islam teaches a dualistic doctrine of Christianity. On one hand it says that the Gospels (Injil) are true, but it also teaches that the Gospels are corrupt (It says the same thing about the Torah).

> Koran 61:6 *And remember when Jesus, son of Mary, said, "Children of Israel! I am Allah's messenger sent to confirm the Law which was already revealed to you and to bring good news of a messenger who will come after me whose name will be Ahmad." [Ahmad was one of Mohammed's*

names. *[This quote of Jesus is not found in any Christian scriptures.] Yet when he [Mohammed] came to them with clear signs, they said, "This is merely sorcery!" And who is more evil than the one who, when called to submit to Islam, makes up a lie about Allah? Allah does not guide the evildoers! They wish to put out Allah's light with their mouths, but as much as the kafirs hate it, Allah will perfect His light.*

THE FINAL STATE OF CHRISTIANS AND JEWS

When Mohammed first started preaching in Mecca, his religion was Arabian. Then Allah became identified with Jehovah and Jewish elements were introduced. When Mohammed moved to Medina, he argued with the Jews when they denied his status as a prophet in the Judaic line. He then annihilated the Jews and makes no more connections between Islam and the Jews. In his last statement, Jews and Christians became perpetual second-class political citizens, dhimmis (those who paid the dhimmi tribute, *jizya,* and were subdued). Only those Christians and Jews who submit to Islam are protected. Islam defines Judaism and Christianity. The real Christians are those who deny the Trinity and accept Mohammed as the final prophet. The real Jews are those who accept Mohammed as the final prophet of their god, Jehovah. Both Christians and Jews must accept that the Koran is the true Scripture and that the Old Testament and New Testament are corrupt and in error. The contradictions between the Koran and the New and Old Testament are proof to Islam of the corruption of the Bible.

All other Jews and Christians are false and kafirs.

> Koran 3:20 *If they argue with you, then say: I have surrendered myself entirely to Allah, as have my followers. Say to the People of the Book and to the ignorant: "Do you surrender to Allah?" If they become Muslims, then they will be guided to the right path, but if they reject it, then your job is only to warn them. Allah watches over all His servants.*

> Koran 9:29 *Make war on those who have received the Scriptures [Jews and Christians] but do not believe in Allah or in the Last Day. They do not forbid what Allah and His Messenger have forbidden. The Christians and Jews do not follow the religion of truth until they submit and pay the poll tax [jizya], and they are humiliated.*

The Christians have hidden their prophecies that Mohammed would come to fulfill the work of Christ. To believe in the divinity of Christ is to refuse to submit to Islam. Those Christians are kafirs and infidels. Like the Jews, only those Christians who submit to Islam and become dhimmis and are ruled by the Sharia (Islamic law) are Christians in the eyes of Islam.

Islam defines all religions. What a Christian says about Jesus and Christianity has no meaning to Islam. Only Islam knows the "real" Christianity.

> Koran 5:72 *The kafirs say, "Jesus is the Messiah, Son of Mary," for the Messiah said, "Oh, Children of Israel, worship Allah, my Lord and your Lord." Whoever will join other gods with Allah, He will forbid him in the Garden, and his abode will be the Fire. The wicked will have no helpers. They surely blaspheme who say, "Allah is the third of three [the Trinity]," for there is no god except one Allah, and if they do not refrain from what they say, a grievous penalty will fall on those who disbelieve. Will they not turn to Allah and ask His forgiveness? For Allah is forgiving and merciful.*
>
> 5:75 *The Messiah, Son of Mary, is but a messenger. Other messengers have passed away before him, and his mother was a saintly woman; they both ate food. See how Allah makes His signs clear to them; then see how they turn from the truth. Say: Will you worship, beside Allah, that which can neither hurt nor help you? Allah hears and knows all things.*

Here is the last mention of Islam and Christianity in the Sira:

Ishaq 903 Mohammed sent Khalid to the fort of a Christian ruler. When the ruler and his brother rode out of their fort to inspect their cattle, Khalid killed the brother and captured the ruler. The ruler agreed to pay the poll tax (jizya) to Islam, and Mohammed returned to Medina.

There is a lot of ink used to say that Christians, Jews and Muslims are all part of the "Abrahamic faith". First of all, the term Abrahamic faith is an Islamic term. It is part of the Meccan Koran that "proves" Islam is true as being an extension of Judaism. The only way a Christian is actually a Christian, according to Islam, is that if the Christian says that Mohammed is the final prophet of God, Christ was a Muslim prophet, the New Testament is corrupt, and there is no Trinity. Only those Christians who admit this are members of the Abrahamic faith. All other Christians are not Christians, but infidels or kafirs.

QUESTIONS

Islam says that the Christian Gospels are corrupt and that the true story of Christ is in the Koran. How do you feel about the truth of the Koran?

What happened in the Crucifixion according to the Koran?

When Christians try to convert Muslims they talk about Jesus and the Gospels. Do you see how Mohammed poisoned the well of the Gospels? How effective is this approach?

Muslims say that Islam is a "brother" religion of Christianity. What do you think of that assertion?

If the Gospels are false, and Christ is a prophet of Allah, what is left of Christianity?

THE DHIMMI

Lesson 6

SUMMARY

- Mohammed attacked the Jews of Khaybar. After crushing them, he created the status of dhimmi for the Jews. They lost all of their wealth, but remained to work on the land. They paid half of all they made each year as a tax. Islam became the complete political ruler of the dhimmi.

- Later, when Islam conquered the Christians, the dhimmi status became codified. All of the public space and legal system was Islamic. The Christians had only their homes and church buildings as their space. Dhimmis had almost no legal rights and could not testify in court against a Muslim.

- Over a 1400 year old period, Islamic jihad has killed over 270,000,000 kafirs.

THE DHIMMI

This next story is very important to Christians as well as Jews. One of Mohammed's inventions was the dhimmi. Dhimmis are kafirs who agree to serve Islam. They are second class citizens, actually, semi-slaves.

Ishaq 756 After the treaty of Al Hudaybiya, Mohammed stayed in Medina for about two months before he collected his army and marched to the forts of Khaybar, a community of wealthy Jewish farmers who lived in a village of separate forts about 100 miles from Medina.

Ishaq 759 Mohammed seized the forts one at a time. On the occasion of Khaybar, Mohammed put forth new orders about forcing themselves on captive women. If the woman was pregnant, she was not to be used until after the birth of the child. Nor were any women to be used who were unclean with regards to the Muslim laws about menstruation.

Ishaq 764 Mohammed knew that there was a large treasure hidden somewhere in Khaybar, so he brought forth the Jew who he thought knew the most about it and questioned him. The Jew denied any knowledge. Mohammed told one of his men, "Torture the Jew until you extract what he has." So the Jew was staked on the ground, and a small fire built on his chest to get him to talk. When the man was nearly dead and still would not talk, Mohammed had him released and taken to one of his men who had had a brother killed in the fight. This Muslim got the pleasure of cutting off the tortured Jew's head.

Ishaq 764 At Khaybar Mohammed instituted the first dhimmis. After the best of the goods were taken from the Jews Mohammed left them to work the land. Since his men knew nothing about farming, and the Jews were skilled at it, they worked the land and gave Mohammed half of their profits.

Ishaq 774 There were a total of 1,800 people who divided up the wealth taken from the beaten Jews of Khaybar. A cavalry man got three shares, a foot soldier got one share. Mohammed appointed eighteen chiefs to divide the stolen wealth. Mohammed received his one-fifth before it was distributed.

Mohammed's invention of the dhimmi was the last necessary political element to rule the world. Now the kafir had a place in Islam. The dhimmi was a semi-slave who was not a Muslim and deferred to Islam. Islam ruled every aspect of government, law and custom.

Today we see dhimmitude. When a kafir calls Islam the religion of peace, the kafir is a dhimmi. When universities teach about Islam and don't teach the suffering of the kafirs, the university is a dhimmi organization. Political correctness and multiculturalism are dhimmitude.

CHRISTIAN DHIMMITUDE

When Muslims are weak, they preach that they are "brothers" of Christians and Jews. That is the current status in America. But when Islam is strong, then all Christians and Jews are dhimmis.

This is how it worked in North Africa, the Middle East and Turkey. Islam invaded a Christian nation; conquered the nation and became the ruling class—claiming all the power and the right to receive special tax money, jizya. Here is the Pact of Umar (the second caliph), the laws of dhimmitude:

1. We shall not build, in our cities or in their neighborhood, new monasteries, churches, convents, or monks' cells, nor shall we repair, by day or by night, such of them as fall in ruins or are situated in the quarters of the Muslims.

2. We shall keep our gates wide open for passersby and travelers. We shall give board and lodging to all Muslims who pass our way for three days.

3. We shall not give shelter in our churches or in our dwellings to any spy, nor hide him from the Muslims.

4. We shall not teach the Koran to our children.

5. We shall not manifest our religion publicly nor convert anyone to it. We shall not prevent any of our kin from entering Islam if they wish it.

6. We shall show respect toward the Muslims, and we shall rise from our seats when they wish to sit.

7. We shall not seek to resemble the Muslims by imitating any of their garments.

8. We shall not mount on saddles, nor shall we gird swords nor bear any kind of arms nor carry them on our persons.

9. We shall not engrave Arabic inscriptions on our seals.

10. We shall not sell fermented drinks.

11. We shall clip the fronts of our heads. [An Arabic sign of shame, a beaten man]

12. We shall always dress in the same way wherever we may be, and we shall bind the zunar round our waists.

13. We shall not display our crosses or our books in the roads or markets of the Muslims. We shall use only clappers in our churches very softly. We shall not raise our voices when following our dead. We shall not take slaves who have been allotted to Muslims.

14. We shall not build houses higher than the houses of the Muslims.

Whoever strikes a Muslim with deliberate intent shall forfeit the protection of this pact.

(from Al-Turtushi, *Siraj al-Muluk*, pp. 229-230)[1]

The treaty is part of dualistic ethics. All of public life is Islamic. Only in the home or in the Church was there any Christianity. Over time the Christians become Islamic in public and adopted Islamic attitudes about women, ethics and other customs. Dhimmitude ground down the Christians until they converted. All they had to do was to say: "There is no god but Allah and Mohammed is His prophet" and all of the persecution stopped. This is way that Turkey became 99.7% Islamic.

But the damage does not stop there. Deep within Christians today is a fear and unease that makes them want to avoid Islam. One of the ways to avoid it is to deny it and/or try to get along. This deference is dhimmitude. So even those Christians who are not formal dhimmis have a mental state of dhimmitude.

---

1   A.S. Trittan, *Caliphs and Their Non-Muslim Subjects*, Idarah-i-Delli, 1950, pg. 5-7.

Notice that one of the terms in the treaty of being a dhimmi is to be ignorant ("we will not teach the Koran to our children") about Islam. It is dhimmitude that explains the vast ignorance of Christians about Islam. Dhimmitude is the reason that schools do not teach the history or doctrine of political Islam. Fear and ignorance change a Christian into a dhimmi. But the good news is that knowledge will transform a dhimmi into a kafir.

THE TEARS OF JIHAD

There was a good reason that Christians, Jews, Hindus, Buddhists and Zoroastrians were dhimmis. First the sword gave political power. The political power gave the basis for changing all of the culture.

First jihad used the sword to take central control. Then there would be surges of mass death by riot and military mass murders. These were jihad as well. An ongoing feature of being a dhimmi was the assassinations and annihilations.

The following figures are a rough estimate of the death of non-Muslims by the political act of jihad.

Africa

Eleven million slaves were shipped across the Atlantic and fourteen million were sent to the Islamic nations of North Africa and the Middle East[1]. For every slave captured many others died. Estimates of this collateral damage vary. For twenty-five million slaves delivered to the market, we have the death of about 120 million people. Muslims have always run the wholesale slave trade in Africa.

120 million Africans

Christians

The number of Christians martyred by Islam is nine million.[2] A rough estimate by Raphael Moore in *History of Asia Minor* is that another fifty million died in wars by jihad. So to account for the one million African Christians killed in the 20th century we have—

60 million Christians

---

1. Thomas Sowell, *Race and Culture*, BasicBooks, 1994, p. 188.
2. David B. Barrett, Todd M. Johnson, *World Christian Trends AD 30-AD 2200*, William Carey Library, 2001, p. 230, table 4-10.

Hindus

Koenard Elst in *Negationism in India*[3] gives an estimate of eighty million Hindus killed in the total jihad against India. The country of India today is only half the size of ancient India, due to jihad.

80 million Hindus

Buddhists

Jihad killed the Buddhists in Turkey, Afghanistan, along the Silk Route, and in India. The total is roughly ten million.[4]

10 million Buddhists

This gives a rough estimate of **270,000,000** killed by jihad.

QUESTIONS

We see jihadists beheading their victims. Where does the custom come from?

Imagine that you live under the Treaty of Umar. In the last week, what would be different in your life?

What are the ethics of the Treaty of Umar?

What do you think happens to a people who live under those kinds of laws for centuries?

How many Jews were killed by Hitler? How do you feel about not knowing how many Christians were killed in jihad?

Where are Christians being brutalized by Islam today? Look beyond Africa.

What do Christians, Jews, Hindus, Buddhists, animists and atheists have in common?

---

3. Koenard Elst, *Negationism in India*, Voice of India, New Delhi, 2002, pg. 34.
4. David B. Barrett, Todd M. Johnson, *World Christian Trends AD 30-AD 2200*, William Carey Library, 2001, p. 230, table 4-1.

WOMEN

Lesson 7

SUMMARY

- Islam's dualism manifests in how women must submit to men. Women can be beaten, but in an Islamic way. Women are spiritually and mentally inferior to men. It takes the testimony of two women to equal that of a man.
- The Islamic law, the Sharia, lays out the proper way to beat the wife.

Islam means submission, submission in all things—religion, politics, culture, civilization and male/female roles. Duality means that everything is divided, and submission means that one side of the duality must dominate the other. All Islamic doctrine follows from submission. Indeed, the opposite is true as well; without submission, there is no Islam. Dualism and submission are the very foundation of Islam.

The major duality inside Islam is male/female. There is one set of rules for men and another set of rules from women. If there were no submission, then there would need to be only one rule: men and women would be treated the same. If they are not to be treated the same, then many more rules are needed.

There is only one way in which a woman is held to be superior to a man: if and only if, a woman is a mother, is she held in higher esteem than a man.

On Judgment Day both male and female will be judged on the basis of what they have done. However, since a woman must submit to the man in all things, she will be judged by how well she submitted during her life.

BEATING THE WIFE

Here we have the words of the Koran:

> Koran 4:34 *Allah has made men superior to women because men spend their wealth to support them. Therefore, virtuous women are obedient, and they are to guard their unseen parts as Allah has guarded them. As for women whom you fear will rebel, admonish them first, and then send*

them to a separate bed, and then beat them. But if they are obedient after that, then do nothing further; surely Allah is exalted and great!

When Mohammed gave his last sermon he mentioned beating the wife:

Ishaq 969 Mohammed also told them men had rights over their wives and women had rights over their husbands. The wives were never to commit adultery or act in a provocative manner toward others. If they did, they were to be put in separate rooms and beaten lightly. [Stoning is the penalty in other hadiths.] If they refrained from what was forbidden, they had the right to food and clothing. Men were to lay injunctions on women lightly for they were prisoners of men and had no control over their persons.

Here from the Sira is some more about the rights of a woman:

Ishaq 957 Mohammed sent Muadh to Yemen to proselytize. While he was there he was asked what rights a husband has over the wife. He replied to the woman who asked, "If you went home and found your husband's nose running with pus and blood and you sucked it until it was cleaned, you still would not have fulfilled your husband's rights."

Physical force is always an option in Islam. Notice that in the Sunna is that when a woman gets beaten by her husband, she should not complain. A beating is a measure of his caring. [One woman sued in Sharia court for a judgment that her husband should stop beating her every day. She wanted the court to rule that he should only beat her once a week.]

> Abu Dawud 11, 2141 *Mohammed said: Do not beat Allah's hand-maidens, but when Umar came to Mohammed and said: Women have become emboldened towards their husbands, Mohammed gave permission to beat them. Then many women came round the family of Mohammed complaining against their husbands.*
>
> *So Mohammed said: Many women have gone round Mohammed's family complaining against their husbands. They are not the best among you.*

This hadith determines Islamic social custom and family law about wife beating.

> Abu Dawud 11, 2142 *Mohammed said: A man will not be asked as to why he beat his wife.*

THE NATURAL INFERIORITY OF WOMEN

It is the nature of females that most of those in Hell will be women.

Bukhari 1,4,184 *Mohammed's followers then told him that during his prayer they saw him reach out with his hands and grasp something, and later retreat in horror. Mohammed replied, "I saw Paradise and stretched my hands towards a bunch of fruit, and had I taken it, you would have eaten from it as long as this world remains. I also saw Hellfire, and I have never seen such a terrible sight. I saw that that the majority of the inhabitants were women." When asked why this was so, Mohammed replied, "They are ungrateful to their husbands and to good deeds. Even if you are good to one of them all of your life, whenever she sees some harshness from you she will say, 'I have never seen any good from you.'"*

Mohammed also saw a woman in Hell being clawed by a cat. He learned that she had imprisoned a cat, neither feeding it nor allowing it to seek its own food, until it starved.

Women are less intelligent than men and they are also spiritually inferior to men.

Bukhari 1,2,28 *Once, after offering prayer at Musalla, Mohammed said to the women, "O women! Give alms, as I have seen that the majority of the dwellers of Hell were women." They asked, "Why is it so, O Allah's Apostle?" He replied, "You curse frequently and are ungrateful to your husbands. I have not seen anyone more deficient in intelligence and religion than you. A cautious sensible man could be led astray by some of you."*

The women asked, "O Allah's Apostle! What is deficient in our intelligence and religion?" He replied, "Is not the evidence of two women equal to the witness of one man?" They agreed that this was so. He said, "This is the deficiency in her intelligence. Isn't it true that a woman can neither pray nor fast during her menses?" The women replied that this was so. He said, "This is the deficiency in her religion."

Women cannot help their flaws, so be nice to them.

Bukhari 4,55,548 *Mohammed said, "Treat women nicely, for a women is created from a rib, and is much like one. If you try to straighten a rib, it will break, so I urge you to take care of the women."*

The general principle in Islamic law is that it takes two women to equal one man.

Koran 2:282 *Believers! When you contract a loan for a certain period, write it down, or to be fair, let a scribe write it down. The scribe should not refuse to write as Allah has taught him; therefore, let the scribe record what the debtor dictates being mindful of his duty to Allah and not reducing the amount he owes. If the debtor is ignorant and unable to dictate, let his guardian do so with fairness. Call two men in to witness this, but if two men cannot be found, then call one man and two women whom you see fit to be witnesses. Therefore, if either woman makes an error, the other can correct her.*

Some good advice about camels, slaves and women:

Abu Dawud 11, 2155 *Mohammed said: If one of you marries a woman or buys a slave, he should say: "O Allah, I ask You for the good in her, and in the disposition You have given her; I take refuge in You from the evil in her, and in the disposition You have given her." When he buys a camel, he should take hold of the top of its hump and say the same kind of thing.*

SHARIA LAW

The Hadith, the Sira and the Koran are all the basis of Islamic law, the Sharia. Here we see how Islamic law deals with wife beating. This is a direct quote from the Sharia. The number is part of an outline system used in the code.

DEALING WITH A REBELLIOUS WIFE[1]

When a husband notices signs of rebelliousness in his wife whether in words as when she answers him coldly when she used to do so politely. or he asks her to come to bed and she refuses, contrary to her usual habit; or whether in acts, as when he finds her averse to him when she was previously kind and cheerful), he warns her in words without keeping from her or hitting her, for it may be that she has an excuse.

The warning could be to tell her,

"Fear Allah concerning the rights you owe to me,"

or it could be to explain that rebelliousness nullifies his obligation to support her and give her a turn amongst other wives, or it could be to inform her,

"Your obeying me is religiously obligatory".

---

1. Ahmad Ibn Naqib Al-Misri, *The Reliance of the Traveller, A Classic Manual of Islamic Sacred Law* (Amana Publications, 1994).

If she commits rebelliousness, he keeps from sleeping with her without words, and may hit her, but not in a way that injures her, meaning he may not bruise her, break bones, wound her, or cause blood to flow. It is unlawful to strike another's face. He may hit her whether she is rebellious only once or whether more than once, though a weaker opinion holds that he may not hit her unless there is repeated rebelliousness.

To clarify this paragraph, we mention the following rulings:
(1) Both man and wife are obliged to treat each other kindly and graciously.
(2) It is not lawful for a wife to leave the house except by the permission of her husband, though she may do so without permission when there is a pressing necessity. Nor may a wife permit anyone to enter her husband's home unless he agrees, even their unmarriageable kin. Nor may she be alone with a non-family-member male, under any circumstances.
(3) It is obligatory for a wife to obey her husband as is customary in allowing him full lawful enjoyment of her person.
(4) If the wife does not fulfill one of the above mentioned obligations, she is termed "rebellious," and the husband takes the following steps to correct matters:
    (a) admonition and advice, by explaining the unlawfulness of rebellion, its harmful effect on married life, and by listening to her viewpoint on the matter;
    (b) if admonition is ineffectual, he keeps from her by not sleeping in bed with her, by which both learn the degree to which they need each other;
    (c) if keeping from her is ineffectual, **it is permissible for him to hit her if he believes that hitting her will bring her back to the right path**, though if he does not think so, it is not permissible. His hitting her may not be in a way that injures her and is his last recourse to save the family.

Every line of the Sharia is taken from the Trilogy. Sharia is the law that Islam wants to replace our Constitution. Freedom, equality and democracy are incompatible with Islamic law.

QUESTIONS

How is Islam's treatment of women dualistic?

Islamic women say they are treated well and that Islam assures women their proper rights. What insight does that give you about Islam?

Why will most of the people in Hell be women?

What is the effect of a female child being told from her first days that she is not as intelligent as a man?

What are the effects of a male child being told about how women are inferior?

If a woman's testimony is half that of a man's, then how can a Muslim man be prosecuted if he forces himself on a woman?

Before a husband beats his wife, what are the steps he should take first?

What are the exact rules for how the beating is to be done?

How would you like to live under Sharia law? How do you feel about Islam's intent to replace our man-made constitution?

SLAVES

Lesson 8

SUMMARY

- Slavery is a positive term in Islam. All Muslims are the slaves of Allah. There is not a single negative statement about slavery in Islam.

- Slavery is based upon a detailed ethical code. It is a sin for a slave to escape a Muslim master. Slaves may be used for pleasure.

- Mohammed was involved in every aspect of the slave culture. Islam has taken slaves from every culture. Islam was the basis of the African slave trade and have enslaved Europeans for centuries.

- Christians act as dhimmis on the subject of slavery.

MOHAMMED AND SLAVERY

Mohammed himself was involved in every single aspect of slavery. He had non-believing men killed so their women and children could be made slaves[1]. He gave slaves away for gifts[2]. He owned many slaves, some of them black[3]. He passed around slaves for the purpose of pleasure to his companions, men who were his chief lieutenants[4]. He stood by while others beat slaves[5]. He dictated the rules of Muslims forcing themselves on women slaves after conquest[6]. He captured slaves and wholesaled them to raise money for jihad[7]. One of his favorite partners was a slave, who bore him a

---

1. A. Guillaume, *The Life of Muhammad* (London: Oxford University Press, 1982), 466.
2. Ibid., p. 499.
3. Ibid., p. 516.
4. Ibid., p. 593.
5. Ibid., p. 295.
6. Ibid., p. 496.
7. Ibid., p. 466.

son[8]. He got slaves as gifts from other rulers[9]. The very pulpit he preached from was made by a slave[10]. He ate food prepared by slaves[11]. He was treated medically by a slave[12]. He had a slave tailor[13]. He declared that a slave who ran away from his master would not have his prayers answered[14]. And he approved an owner's forcing himself on his female slaves[15].

The word slave is a positive one in Islam. Every Muslim is a slave of Allah. Mohammed was involved with every conceivable aspect of slavery. The word Islam means submission and a slave is the ultimate expression of submission.

> Koran 2:23 *If you doubt what We have revealed to Our slave [Mohammed], then write a sura comparable to it and call your gods other than Allah to help you if what you say is true.*

Bukhari has 42 references to Mohammed as the Slave of Allah.

> [Bukhari 4,55,654] *Umar heard the Prophet saying, "Do not exaggerate in praising me as the Christians praised the son of Mary, for I am only a slave. So, call me the Slave of Allah and His Apostle."*

Slavery is as natural as breathing in Islam. The word is never used in a negative way in the Koran, Sira or Hadith. Slavery is in the Sunna of Mohammed and part of the Koran.

Slaves are part of the natural order of society.

> Koran 16:71 *Allah has given more of His gifts of material things to some rather than others. In the same manner, those who have more do not give an equal share to their slaves so that they would share equally. Would they then deny the favors of Allah?*

DUALITY AND SUBMISSION

Duality is the only way to sustain slavery, and Islam has sustained slavery for 1400 years. A believer, a Muslim, may not be enslaved. Only the kafirs can be enslaved. The duality of believer/kafir divides all humanity. The kafirs are fair game and can be attacked, their protectors killed, their

---

8. William Muir, *The Life of Mohammed* (AMS Press, 1975), 425.
9. Ibid., p. 425.
10. Bukhari, Hadith, Volume 1, Book 8, Number 440.
11. Ibid., Volume 3, Book 34, Number 295.
12. Ibid., Volume 3, Book 36, Number 481.
13. Ibid., Volume 7, Book 65, Number 344.
14. Muslim, Hadith, Book 001, Number 0131.
15. Ibid., Book 008, Number 3383.

wealth taken and the remaining people enslaved. Slavery is Allah's way. If the slave converts to Islam, then freedom is a possibility.

Slavery can be part of the sacred order of Islam since duality is the very basis of Islam. There is one set of rules for Muslims and another set of rules for the kafirs. The only unifying rule in Islam is that every single human being must submit to Islam. Before that submission, the Muslim and the kafir have nothing in common.

Slavery is a supreme example of Islam's dualistic ethics and submission. Who submits more than a slave?

Freeing slaves has great merit and is approved in both the Koran and the Hadith. However, only slaves who convert are freed. So here we see the great power of Islamic slavery. Those who are slaves will become Muslims in order to be freed. If they don't then their children will.

However, merely converting to Islam after being enslaved does not mean the slave is to be freed. Converting is the first step, but the owner may, or may not, free the converted slave.

In the next verse, Allah gives Islam power over its captives.

> Koran 8:70 *Messenger! Tell the captives who are under your control, "If Allah finds good in your hearts [if the prisoners convert to Islam], He will give you something better than that which has been taken away from you, and He will show you forgiveness. Truly, Allah is forgiving and merciful." If, however, they plot to betray you, know that they have already betrayed Allah. He has therefore given you power over them. Allah is all-knowing and wise.*

For a slave to flee his Islamic master is a sin against Allah.

> Muslim 001,0131 *Mohammed: "If a slave flees his master, Allah does not hear his prayer."*

For a Muslim to have pleasure with his slaves is in the same moral category as being humble, telling the truth or giving to charity. There is no blame and it is a moral good. Forcing themselves on slaves is only good for the male Muslim. Of course, for the female Muslim it is forbidden for her to lay with a kafir slave.

> Koran 4:24 *Also forbidden to you are married women unless they are your slaves. This is the command of Allah. Other than those mentioned, all other women are lawful to you to court with your wealth and with honorable intentions, not with lust. And give those you have slept with a dowry, as it is your duty. But after you have fulfilled your duty, it is not an offense to make additional agreements among you. Truly Allah is knowing and wise!*

The above verse was given at the time of the jihad at Khaybar. Mohammed attacked the Jews of Khaybar and conquered them. The Jews that survived were doomed to become *dhimmis*. A dhimmi is not a Muslim, but one who has agreed to do all things as Islam wishes. In this case the surviving Jews were to work the land and give half of the proceeds to the jihadists. In addition, some women were taken as slaves of pleasure.

Ishaq 758 [This event is right after the capture of Khaybar.] Dihya had asked Mohammed for Safiya, and when he chose her for himself Mohammed gave Safiya's two cousins to Dihya in exchange. *The women of Khaybar were distributed among the Muslims.*

Ishaq 759 A man said, 'Let me tell you what I heard the apostle say on the day of Khaybar. He got up among us and said: "It is not lawful for a Muslim *to mingle his seed with another man's [meaning violating a pregnant woman among the captives], nor is it lawful for him to take her until he has made sure that she is in a state of cleanness [not having her period].*

The violation of women during jihad is a constant in the Hadith and the Sira.

HISTORY

If you live in America, you know the modern historical theory of slavery. Evil white men brought Africans to the Western hemisphere, where they were sold for profit and put to work as slaves. The modern theory is true as far as it goes, but it does not go nearly far enough. Slavery goes far beyond the 300-year period during which whites bought slaves from the Muslim wholesalers on the West coast of Africa.

Every culture has had some form of slavery in its past. Slavery is an answer to how to get hard, rough work done. We feel ethically superior to our ancestors because we don't have slaves. But the reason that slavery was finally ended was a combination of ethics and the discovery of a better slave—the machine.

White Slaves

For 1400 years—until the slave market was officially closed in the early 1960s—the highest priced slave in Mecca was the white woman. The price of a white slave girl was from three to ten times that of a black girl. When Islam invaded Spain, the first thing exported back to Islamic North Africa was a thousand blond-haired girls.

Our word for slave comes from the Slavs of eastern Europe. So many of them were taken by the Muslims of the Ottoman Empire that the very term *Slav* came to mean slave. And black slaves were so numerous that the term *abd* came to mean black or African. Muslims called the white slaves *mamluk*.

Not only were the words for slaves different, but the uses of them were different. The white woman was favored for pleasure. That is why she brought the best price. White slaves were not used for rough labor but were used for higher positions in domestic and administrative work. Both white and black eunuchs were used in the harem.

There is an interesting aspect to castration in Islam. White male slaves were simply castrated; whereas, black slaves were completely surgically altered.

Black Slaves

About 11 million slaves were shipped across the Atlantic, and 14 million were sent to the Islamic nations of North Africa and the Middle East[1]. For every slave captured, many others died. Estimates of this collateral damage vary. The renowned missionary David Livingstone estimated that for every slave who reached the plantation, five others died by being killed in the raid or died on the forced march from illness and privation[2]. Those who were left behind were the very young, the weak, the sick and the old. These soon died since the main providers had been killed or enslaved. So, for 25 million slaves delivered to the market, we have the death of about 120 million people. Islam ran the wholesale slave trade in Africa from the time of Mohammed.

DHIMMITUDE

Historically, Muslims are dominant over every other demographic group. No one is lower than a slave. No one is higher than the slave's master. For 1400 years Islam has enslaved African, Asians, Christians, Hindus, Buddhists, Europeans and even Americans. On the other hand, no one enslaves Muslims, unless the African slaver runs out of kafirs. But even then, it is a Muslim who enslaves the Muslim.

The absolute dominance of the Muslim today is shown by the fact that no one blames them or holds them responsible for slavery. Islam not only enslaves the bodies of the kafirs, but enslaves the minds of the kafir intellectuals. One of the most forbidden topics to be discussed is the role of Islam in slavery, both today and throughout the last 1400 years.

---

1. Thomas Sowell, *Race and Culture*, BasicBooks, 1994, p. 188.
2. Woman's Presbyterian Board of Missions, *David Livingstone,* p. 62, 1888.

As a cruel example of how the kafir mind submits to Islam regarding slavery, go to an event where freed slaves from Africa or the "Lost Boys" of the Sudan are featured. Money is raised, sympathy is given and not one word about Islam is ever mentioned. Slavery just happens. We get to see an effect without a cause, an impossibility, but a false reality, nevertheless.

This mental submission of the kafir to Islam is dhimmitude. There are three ways to submit to the duality of Islam. The first is to be a Muslim. The second is to be a slave. But Mohammed invented a third way of submission—the dhimmi.

When the kafir lets Islam have its way in public affairs, the kafir becomes a dhimmi. When kafirs teach about slavery and don't teach about Islam and slavery, the kafir is a dhimmi. When the university curriculum about "gender studies" does not include the servitude of the Islamic woman, the mind set of the curriculum is dhimmitude. When the rabbi or the minister says that he worships the same god as the Muslim, but have never read the Trilogy, the rabbi and the ministers are dhimmis. When the media report or talk about Islam and have no knowledge about the doctrine or history of political Islam, they are dhimmis.

QUESTIONS

How is slavery dualistic?

The idea of a white slave master forcing himself on a slave is abhorrent to us. Why do we never hear about Muslim masters and their slaves of pleasure? Why don't we know that white women were the slave of choice in the Meccan slave market?

Why don't we ever talk about Mohammed and slavery? Why don't we even know about it?

Christians have been subject to Islamic slavery for a thousand years. Why don't we study that history?

Christians in Islamic Eastern Europe [Turkey ruled large parts of Eastern Europe for centuries.] had to "give" a son to the Sultan to be raised as a Muslim slave soldier to be used against Christians. How would you feel about paying such a tax?

ETHICS

Lesson 9

SUMMARY

- Islamic ethics are dualistic. Islam has one code for believers and a second ethical code for kafirs. The term kafir is dualistic, since the kafir is the "other". Jihad and slavery all have an Islamic ethical code.

- A Muslim is a brother only to other Muslims. A Muslim is honest with other Muslims and may deceive kafirs. There is an Islamic word for sacred deception, *taqiyya.*

- Killing a kafir is not a serious charge in Islamic law. Theft and murder are acceptable in Islam.

Ethics is at the root of every human action and underlies our motivation. Ethics determines our point-of-view. Fundamentally, there are only two ethical systems. The first is based upon the ideal of

Do unto others as you would have them do unto you.

This idea is called the Golden Rule and is found in most cultures. This ethic is based upon the idea that others are fundamentally the same as ourselves. This does not mean we are equal in abilities. Any teacher or coach knows that. It is a unitary ethical system, since it sees humanity as one spirit and one ethical body.

Everyone wants to be treated as a human being. In particular, we all want to be equal under the law and be treated as social equals. On the basis of the Golden Rule—the equality of human beings—we have created democracy, ended slavery and treat women and men as political equals. So the Golden Rule is a unitary ethic. All people are to be treated the same. All religions have some version of the Golden Rule except Islam.

Now mind you, kafirs have frequently failed at applying the Golden Rule, but they can be judged and condemned on its basis. They may fall short, but it is the ideal.

DUALISTIC ETHICS

There is another basis for ethics—dualism. In dualistic thought there is no such thing as a unified humanity, but a division into two parts: them and us. Much of the Trilogy is devoted to establishing the division between Islam and the kafir.

At a political level, the duality manifests as:

dar al Islam, land of submission
dar al harb, land of war

Duality is the very basis of Islam's ethics. It could not be any other way. Islam's ethics are based upon on the Koran and the Sunna of Mohammed. Over half of the Koran deals with the division between Islam and the kafir. The Koran is based upon duality.

There is no such thing as a universal statement of ethics in Islam. Muslims are to be treated one way and kafirs another way. The closest Islam comes to a universal statement of ethics is that the entire world must submit to Islam. After Mohammed became a prophet, he never treated a kafir the same as a Muslim. Islam denies the truth of the Golden Rule.

The term "human being" has no meaning inside of Islam. There is no such thing as humanity, only the duality of the believer and kafir. In the ethical statements found in the Hadith, a Muslim should not lie, cheat, kill or steal from other Muslims. But a Muslim may lie, deceive or kill a kafir if it advances Islam.

Every action and word of Mohammed was based upon whether he was dealing with a Muslim or a kafir. Mohammed's every action and word as recorded in the Sira and Hadith, define Islamic ethics. It is impossible for an action or word of Mohammed to be unethical.

Mohammed's ethics were dualistic. Therefore, Islam's ethics are dualistic.

Islam's ethics are supremely powerful and effective in politics. Dualism is the foundation of jihad, dhimmitude and slavery.

There is not one sentence in the Trilogy that has the slightest sympathy for the suffering of the kafir. Mohammed never once expressed any regret at the torture, killing, enslavement, humiliation of kafir men by the violation of kafir women. The suffering of the kafir is defined as good. The Koran is ecstatic at the suffering of the kafir. Indeed, the finest poetic imagery of the Koran is reserved for the torture and suffering of the kafir. The kafir is pure "other," and Islam cannot be too deceptive or too cruel to the kafir.

Mohammed's response to the heads of the kafirs thrown at his feet was pure joy.

KAFIR

Kafir defines the ethical dualism of Islam at a personal level. To call someone a kafir is an ethical statement.

A Muslim may be friendly to a kafir if it advances Islam, but he is not actually a friend. A kafir is not a real human; Muslims are the only real humans. The only good in a kafir is how the kafir can serve or enrich Islam.

SLAVERY

Slavery, like jihad, is the logical conclusion to dualistic ethics. Slavery was used by Mohammed for very simple reasons. He had known slavery from his first breath. There was never a Mohammed without slavery. Slaves were as common as camels in Arabia. Slaves were a free source of energy, power and money. And the slaves eventually became Muslims.

For Mohammed, slavery was totally positive. Allah said so. Just treat the slaves well. Men forcing themselves on female slaves was part of the good treatment of slaves. This is pure dualism. When Muslims violated the women of the conquered tribes after killing their men, we find no empathy or compassion, only the triumph of dualism. A Muslim's *ghira*, maleness, power and prestige, is increased with this treatment of the inferior kafir woman. Dualism transforms this into a sacred good.

Slavery is good. All Muslims are slaves of Allah. So the enslavement of others enriches Islam and helps to Islamicize the kafir world.

The ethics of dualistic slavery can be seen in Islam's attitude toward the history of slavery. Islam never acknowledges its role in the history of the suffering of slavery. Islam has no regrets or guilt about slavery.

THE ETHICS OF KILLING AND DECEPTION

Kafir, jihad, dualism and slavery are the results of a very detailed system of ethics. Islamic ethics determines what is truth, honesty, how to treat Muslims and how to treat the kafir. All of these underlie the ability of Islam to carry out jihad, slavery and kafir submission. Everything in Islam is directed towards submission and is based upon a dualistic system of thought.

Dualistic ethics that defines brotherhood, honesty, truth and the legal system makes it possible to kill, enslave, deceive, and cheat the kafir.

BROTHERHOOD

The brother of a Muslim is another Muslim.

> Bukhari 1,2,12 *Mohammed: "True faith comes when a man's personal desires mirror his wishes for other Muslims."*

> Bukhari 9,85,83 *Mohammed: "A Muslim is a brother to other Muslims. He should never oppress them nor should he facilitate their oppression. Allah will satisfy the needs of those who satisfy the needs of their brothers."*

HONESTY

A Muslim should always be honest in dealing with other Muslims.

> Bukhari 3,34,301 *A man selling wares in the market place swore by Allah that he had been offered a certain price for his goods when, in fact, no such offer existed. He lied about the offer to drive up the price for his goods and thus cheat a fellow Muslim. Consequently, this verse in the Koran was revealed to Mohammed:*

> Koran 3:77 Those who sell their covenant with Allah and their oaths for a meager price will have no part in the world to come. Allah will not find them worthy to speak to or even glance in their direction on the Day of Resurrection, nor will He forgive them. They will have a painful end.

TRUTH

In Islam something that is not true is not always a lie.

> Bukhari 3,49,857 *Mohammed: "A man who brings peace to the people by making up good words or by saying nice things, though untrue, does not lie."*

A Muslim's oath is flexible.

> Bukhari 8,78,618 *Abu Bakr faithfully kept his oaths until Allah revealed to Mohammed the atonement for breaking them. Afterwards he said, "If I make a pledge and later discover a more worthy pledge, then I will take the better action and make amends for my earlier promise."*

When deception advances Islam, the deception is not a sin. Ali was Mohammed's nephew and was raised by him from the age of ten and became the fourth caliph. Ali pronounced the following on lies and deception.

Bukhari 9,84,64 *When I relate to you the words of Mohammed, by Allah, I would rather die than bear false witness to his teachings. However, if I should say something unrelated to the prophet, then it might very well be a lie so that I might deceive my enemy. Without question, I heard Mohammed say, "In the final days before Redemption there will emerge groups of foolish youths who will say all the right things but their faith will go no further than their mouths and will flee from their religion like an arrow. So, kill the apostates wherever you find them, because whoever does so will be rewarded on Judgment Day."*

Deceit is permissible in jihad:

Muslim 032,6303 *According to Mohammed, someone who strives to promote harmony amongst the faithful and says or conveys good things is not a liar. Ibn Shihab said that he had heard only three exceptions to the rules governing false statements: lies are permissible in war, to reconcile differences between the faithful, and to reconcile a husband and wife through the manipulation or twisting of words.*

Taqiyya is deception that advances Islam. A lie should never be told unless there is no other way to accomplish the task. Al Tabarani, in Al Awsat, said, "Lies are sins except when they are told for the welfare of a Muslim or for saving him from a disaster." [1]

An example of sacred deceit, *taqiyya*:

Ishaq 224 A member of the Abyssinian royalty, called the Negus, became convinced of the truth of Islam. He was accused by the Christians of leaving his religion. The Negus wrote on a piece of paper, "There is no god but Allah and Mohammed is his prophet. Jesus was a Muslim, born of Mary, conceived without a father." [These are classical Islamic statements.] He the then pinned the statement under his shirt over his heart. When the other Abyssinians accused the Negus of leaving Christianity and they said, "Jesus was the Son of God." The Negus placed his hand over his heart (and the paper with the statement) and told the Christians, "I testify that Jesus was no more than this." The Christians took him at his word and left him. When Mohammed heard this, he prayed for the Negus when he died.

---

1. Bat Ye'or, *The Dhimmi* (Cranbury, N.J.: Associated University Presses, 2003), 392.

LAW

The hadiths are the basis of the Sharia, Islamic law. Here is a hadith about capital crimes. Killing a non-Muslim is not a capital crime.

> Bukhari 1,3,111 *I [Abu] asked Ali, "Do you know of any sources of law that were revealed to Mohammed other than the Koran?" Ali responded, "None except for Allah's law, or the ability of reason given by Allah to a Muslim, or these written precepts I possess." I said, "What are these written rules?" Ali answered, "They concern the blood money paid by a killer to a victim's relatives, the method of ransoming a captive's release from the enemy, and the law that a Muslim must never be killed as punishment for killing a non-Muslim."*

TREATMENT OF FELLOW MUSLIMS

Weapons in the mosque are acceptable. The mosque is a political center as well as a community center and a place of worship.

> Bukhari 1,8,443 *Mohammed: "Arrows should be held by their heads when carried through mosques or markets so that they do not harm a Muslim."*

> Bukhari 9,88,193 *Mohammed: "You should not aim your weapons at other Muslims; you never know, Satan might tempt you to harm them, and your sin would send you to Hell."*

Killing a Muslim is a crime.

> Koran 25:68 *They do not call upon other gods along with Allah and do not kill those whom Allah has forbidden to be killed [other Muslims] except for just cause.*

> Koran 4:93 *For those who intentionally kill another Muslim, Hell will be their punishment, where they will live forever. The wrath of Allah will be upon them, He will curse them, and they will receive terrible torture.*

In business, a Muslim should never cheat a Muslim.

> Bukhari 9,86,109 *Mohammed said, "A neighbor has a greater expectation of help from his neighbor[2] than anyone else." Some said, "If a man wants to buy a house there is no harm done if he uses*

---

2.   Other hadiths show that neighbor meant other Muslims who lived in their own neighborhoods.

trickery to prevent another from buying it." Abu Abdullah said, "*So that man says that some people are allowed to play tricks on other Muslims though Mohammed said, 'When doing business with other Muslims do not sell them sick animals or defective or stolen goods.'*"

Bukhari 8,73,70 *Mohammed: "Harming a Muslim is an evil act; killing a Muslim means rejecting Allah."*

POSITION TOWARD OTHER RELIGIONS

Mohammed's deathbed wishes were to create religious apartheid in Arabia and to use money to influence kafirs for Islam.

Bukhari 4,52,288 *[...]* "*On his deathbed Mohammed gave three final orders saying, 'First, drive the non-Muslims from Arabia. Second, give gifts and show respect to foreign officials as I have done.' I forgot the third command."*

THEFT

Taking the wealth of the kafir is sanctioned by the Koran as the legalization of booty.

Bukhari 1,7,331 *Mohammed said, "I have been given five things which were not given to any one else before me.*

1. Allah made me victorious by awe, by His frightening my enemies for a distance of one month's journey.

2. The earth has been made for me and for my followers a place for praying and a place for our rituals.

3. The booty of war has been made lawful for me yet it was not lawful for anyone else before me.

4. I have been given the right of intercession on the Day of Resurrection.

5. Every Prophet used to be sent to his nation only but I have been sent to all mankind.

FORCING THEMSELVES ON WOMEN

The abuse of women after jihad is a constant in the Hadith and the Sira. Here we see that at first the jihadists were reluctant to force themselves on the captive women because of their husbands being nearby. But the Koran established that it was not immoral even if they had husbands.

Muslim 008, 3432 *Mohammed sent an army to Autas and encountered the enemy and fought with them. Having overcome them and taken them captives, the Companions seemed to refrain from forcing themselves on captive women because of their husbands being polytheists. Then Allah, Most High, sent down regarding that: "And women already married, except those whom your right hands possess[1] (iv. 24)" (i. e. they were lawful for them when their menstral period came to an end).*

Forcing themselves on women is used in jihad because it works as a tactic of war. It spreads shame among the kafir men and women and it begins the process of subjugating the kafir women. In short, it teaches everybody their place in Islam—submission.

A CONCLUSION

There is no hadith that ever refers to humanity as one body. Every hadith that refers to humanity is dualistic—divided into Muslims and kafirs. Islamic ethics are completely dualistic.

Islamic ethics have no place for integrity. Indeed, integrity is not possible within any dualistic system. Integrity cannot be logically defined within a dualistic system. If deceit is a virtue, then integrity is not a possibility.

No one who adheres to Islamic ethics can have integrity. They cannot tell the kafir the whole truth and nothing but the truth, about Islam.

QUESTIONS

What are dualistic ethics?

Would you want to work with someone who has dualistic ethics?

Why does dualistic ethics make Islam so powerful?

How is the word kafir a slur and bigoted?

Why are dualistic ethics so confusing?

A Muslim soldier or cop has sworn an oath to "serve and protect". How would you feel about serving with him?

---

1   The right hand is the sword hand. The phrase comes from the Koran.

A Muslim doctor has sworn to the Hippocratic oath. What does that mean if he is working with a kafir?

How can a kafir have equal protection under the law in a Muslim country?

Theft comes in many forms. We call our numbers, Arabic numerals. But the Arabs got the mathematics and the numbers, including the concept of zero, from their Hindu dhimmis. Why do we honor the theft by calling the Hindu numerals Arabic numerals?

What does the Golden Rule mean in Islam?

SELECTIONS FROM THE KORAN

Lesson 10

SUMMARY

· Islamic Paradise is a garden of fleshly pleasures.

· There are creatures, similar to spirits, called jinns that populate the earth.

· Allah determines all things, including whether a person becomes a Muslim. Allah creates some men for Hell.

· The Koran is filled with violence.

· The Koran contradicts itself but has rules for dealing with the contradictions.

· Allah is to be feared, not loved.

EVERYDAY

The following verses are repeated daily by every Muslim. The first four verses are a standard piousness. But notice that verse 5 says that the Jews anger Allah and that the Christians are wrong.

> Koran 1:1 *In the Name of Allah, the Compassionate, the Merciful.*
> 1:2 *Praise be to Allah, Lord of the worlds. The Compassionate, the Merciful. King of the Judgment Day.*
> 1:5 *Only You do we worship, and to You alone do we ask for help. Keep us on the straight and narrow path. The path of those that You favor; not the path of those who anger You [the Jews] nor the path of those who go astray [the Christians].*

HEAVEN/HELL

Islamic Paradise (it is never called Heaven) is a place where a man can have all the pleasure he wants with virgins, drink wine and never get a hangover, eat all he wants and watch the people in Hell be tortured and taunt them.

> Koran 56:11 *A few of those who lived later [after Islam was well established] will be on decorated couches, reclining on them face to face. They*

will be waited on by immortal young boys with goblets and ewers and a cup of pure wine that gives no headache nor muddles the mind, and with fruits that are most pleasing, and with the flesh of birds that they desire. In compensation for their past good deeds, they will have houris [heavenly companions of pleasure] with big, dark eyes like pearls peeking from their shells. They will not hear any vain or sinful talk, only the cry, "Peace! Peace!"

56:27 *The people of the right-hand—Oh! How happy the people of the right-hand will be resting on raised couches amid thornless sidrahs [plum trees] and talh trees [banana trees], thick with fruit, and in extended shade and constantly flowing waters, and abundant fruits, neither forbidden nor out of reach. And We have specially made for them houris, companions, chaste and pure virgins, lovers and friends of equal age with them for the people of the right hand, a large number of the people of old, and a large number of the people of the latter generations.*

Koran 55:56 *There will be bashful virgins who gaze modestly, who have never been touched by either man nor jinn. Which of your Lord's blessings would you deny?*

The most expressive language of the Koran is reserved for Hell.

Koran 4:56 *Those who reject Our revelations We will cast into the Fire. As soon as their skins are burnt away, We will give them new skins so that they will truly experience the torment. Truly Allah is mighty and wise!*

OATHS

Allah swears oaths in the Koran. Why does Allah swear? Simple, Arabs swore oaths to establish the truth.

Koran 51:5 *Truly, that which threatens you [the Meccans] is real. The Judgment will certainly happen. I [Allah] swear by the star-tracked heaven!*

JINNS

The Koran is very clear that there are spirits called jinns who are here on earth. Jinns are made of fire. Most of them cause evil, but some are religious. We get the name genie from the name jinn.

Koran 72:1 *Say: It has been revealed to me that a group of jinn listened [to Mohammed recite the Koran] and said, "Truly, we have heard a wonderful recital. It guides us to the truth. We believe in it, and we will never again worship another god. Exalted is the majesty of Our Lord! He has neither a wife nor a child. The foolish among us speak of a god that is unjust. We believed that no man or jinn would utter a lie against Allah."*

Koran 46:29 *We sent a company of jinn so that they might hear the Koran. When the reading was finished, they returned to their people with warnings. They said, "Oh, people! We have heard a scripture sent down since the days of Moses verifying previous scriptures, a guide to the truth and the straight path. Oh, people! Hear the Messenger of Allah and believe Him that He will forgive your faults and protect you from tormenting punishment."*

PREDESTINATION

The Koran is a dualistic text. Allah constantly admonishes the world to do what Mohammed says. But then it also says again and again that Allah causes men to err.

Koran 42:44 *Whomever Allah sends astray will no longer have a protector.*

Koran 6:25 *Some among them listen to you [Mohammed], but We have cast veils over their hearts and a heaviness to their ears so that they cannot understand our signs [the Koran].*

Koran 32:13 *If We had wished, We could have given guidance to every soul. My word will come true: "I will fill Hell with jinns and men together. So taste the evil of your deeds. You forgot that you would have a meeting on Judgment Day. We will forget you. Taste the eternal punishment because of your actions.*

Koran 14:4 *We have only sent a messenger who speaks the language of his own people [Arabic] so that he might speak clearly to them. But Allah misleads whom He will and guides whom He will. He is mighty and wise.*

PLOTTING

The Koran repeatedly says that Allah plots and schemes against the kafirs.

Koran10:21 *When We grant men a mercy after an adversity has afflicted them and We cause this people to taste of mercy, they start plotting against Our signs. Say: Allah is swifter to plot. Our messengers record all the plots you make.*

VIOLENCE

Koran 33:60 *If the hypocrites, the men with diseased hearts and the troublemakers in Medina, do not desist, We will raise you up against them and they will not remain in the city much longer. They will be cursed, and wherever they are found, they will be seized and murdered. It was*

Allah's same practice with those who came before them, and you will find no change in Allah's ways.

Koran 4:47 **To those of you [Jews and Christians] to whom the Scriptures were given: Believe in what We have sent down confirming the Scriptures you already possess before We destroy your faces and twist your heads around backwards, or curse you as We did those [the Jews] who broke the Sabbath for Allah's commandments will be carried out.**

The Koran mentions iron twice, both times as a use in war.

Koran 57:25 **We have sent Our messengers with clear signs, and We have caused the Scriptures and the balance of justice to come down through them. We have sent down iron with its strength for war as well as its many other uses for mankind so that Allah would know those who would help Him and His messengers, although unseen. Allah is powerful and mighty.**

ABROGATION

The Koran contradicts itself. When verses contradict, then the later verses are to be used. However, the earlier verses can still be used, since the later verses are better, but the earlier verses are still true. This abrogation is at the root of the dualistic nature of the Koran.

Koran 2:106 **Whatever of Our revelations We repeal or cause to be forgotten, We will replace with something superior or comparable. [There are as many as 225 verses of the Koran that are altered by later verses, abrogation.] Do you not know that Allah has power over all things? Do you not know that Allah reigns sovereign over the heavens and earth and besides Him you have no protector or helper?**

FEAR

There are over 300 verses in the Koran that say humanity is to fear Allah.

Koran 3:101 **Believers! Fear Allah as He deserves to be feared! When death finds you, die as true Muslims.**

MOHAMMED'S FAMILY LIFE

Mohammed's family life is mentioned many times in the Koran. Also, notice that Mohammed's oaths are flexible. Therefore, so are all Islamic oaths flexible. That is the nature of the Sunna.

Koran 66:1 *Why, Oh, Messenger, do you forbid yourself that which Allah has made lawful to you? Do you seek to please your wives?* [Mohammed was fond of a Coptic (Egyptian Christian) slave of pleasure named Mary. Hafsa found Mohammed in her room with Mary, a violation of Hafsa's domain. He told a jealous Hafsa that he would stop relations with Mary and then did not. But Hafsa was supposed to be quiet about this matter.] *Allah is lenient and merciful. Allah has allowed you release from your oaths, and Allah is your master. He is knowing and wise.*

Marriage to his daughter-in-law:

Koran 33:36 *And it is not the place of a believer, either man or woman, to have a choice in his or her affairs when Allah and His Messenger have decided on a matter. Those who disobey Allah and His Messenger are clearly on the wrong path. And remember when you said to your adopted son [Zaid], the one who had received Allah's favor [converted to Islam], "Keep your wife to yourself and fear Allah," and you hid in your heart what Allah was to reveal, and you feared men [what people would say if he married his daughter-in-law], when it would have been right that you should fear Allah. And when Zaid divorced his wife, We gave her to you as your wife, so it would not be a sin for believers to marry the wives of their adopted sons, after they have divorced them. And Allah's will must be carried out.*

DUALITY

Any verse in the Koran which seems to advocate good towards the kafir is always compromised somewhere else. Here is a well known verse:

Koran 5:32 *For this reason, We have decreed to the Children of Israel that whoever kills anyone, unless it is manslaughter, or for spreading mischief in the land, it will be as though he had slain all mankind. Whoever saves a life, it will be as though he had saved all mankind. Certainly Our messengers came to them [the Jews] with the proofs of their mission, and even after this, most of them committed excesses in the land.*

When President Bush read this statement after 9/11, he only quoted the "that whoever kills anyone, unless it is manslaughter, or for spreading mischief in the land, it will be as though he had slain all mankind. Whoever saves a life, it will be as though he had saved all mankind." But that law only applies to the Jews. Then read the next verse:

Koran 5:33 *The only reward for those who war against Allah and His messengers and strive to commit mischief on the earth is that they will be slain or crucified, have their alternate hands and feet cut off, or be banished from the land. This will be their disgrace in this world, and a great*

71

torment shall be theirs in the next except those who repent before you overpower them. Know that Allah is forgiving and merciful.

Thus Koran 5:32 does not abjure violence, instead it makes clear that anyone opposing Islam will be killed, crucified, mutilated, or banished.

Here is another example of dualism. Sura 109 sounds just wonderfully tolerant:

Koran 109:1 *Say: Oh you unbelievers! I do not worship what you worship, and you do not worship what I worship. I will never worship what you worship, and you will never worship what I worship. You to your religion, me to my religion.*

But here we have a later verse that abrogates it (Sura 9 is the last sura):

Koran 9:123 *Believers, fight the unbelievers who are near you, and let them find you to be tough and hard. Know that Allah is with those who guard against evil.*

So Islam uses the "good" verses when needed, but always has a secret weapon, the "bad" verses, hidden for use when needed.

QUESTIONS

We say that prayer is good. Is the prayer of Sura 1 a good prayer?

How would you describe Paradise?

Have you met any jinns lately?

You are not a Muslim. How do you feel about the fact that is Allah's choice?

If the Koran is filled with contradictions, what does that say about Allah? Why couldn't Allah get it right the first time?

How does it make you feel to know that Mohammed's favorite slave of pleasure was a Christian?

If the Koran is dualistic, what does that say about Allah?

Some Christians use the Koran to try to prove that the Gospels are good. Why would a Christian use any part of the Koran to prove anything about Christianity?

SUBMISSION AND DUALITY

Lesson 11

SUMMARY

- Islam is based upon two principles—submission and duality. All of the world's civilizations, cultures and political systems must submit to Islam.

- Duality means that Islam always divides everything in two. It also holds two contradictory positions on nearly every topic. Even though the ideas contradict, they are both true.

- Submission means that Islam must dominate all aspects of humanity. Art, literature, education, customs, food, law and every other aspect of being a human must be done in the way of Islam.

There are two principles to Islam—submission and duality.

"Islam" is an Arabic word that means submission. A Muslim is one who has submitted to Allah. Submission is a statement of power with one thing dominant over the other. As long as it is a religious statement then the rest of the world has no problem. However, since Islam is a political system, submission is the relation between Islam and the kafirs. We see this as Muslims come to America. Our institutions must submit to Islam. Schools must teach a history that Islam approves of. Newspapers cannot publish the Danish cartoons of Mohammed because Islam demands that out freedom of the press must submit to Islam. Everything, over time, in the public sphere must conform to the principles of Islam.

Islam has very long term political goals and is infinitely patient. Islam's goals in America are very simple. Our Constitution is an affront to Allah and is man-made. Over the long term it must submit to Sharia law, Islamic law. From the standpoint of Islam, this is only just. All man-made governments are inherently evil and a work of ignorance. The dualism of political Islam is seen in Muslims who say they love America and the Constitution, all the while working to end the American culture.

Sometimes you hear that Islam means peace. The peace of Islam comes only after you submit to Islam. Here we see how Christians have peace under Islam:

> Koran 9:29 *Make war on those who have received the Scriptures [Jews and Christians] but do not believe in Allah or in the Last Day. They do not forbid what Allah and His Messenger have forbidden. The Christians and Jews do not follow the religion of truth until they submit and pay the poll tax [jizya], and they are humiliated.*

Islam means submission and then there is peace. Inside Islam women must submit to the males. Outside Islam, the kafirs must submit. Islam's doctrine of slavery is based upon submission.

DUALITY

Submission is an unpleasant concept, but it is easy to understand. Duality is unique to Islam. Dualism is the foundation and key to understanding Islam.

Our first clue about the dualism is in the Koran. The insight into the logic of the Koran comes from the large numbers of contradictions in it. Both sides of the contradiction are true in dualistic logic. The circumstances govern which verse is used.

For example:

> Koran 73:10 *Listen to what they [unbelievers] say with patience, and leave them with dignity.*

From tolerance we move to the ultimate intolerance—not even the Lord of the Universe can stand the kafirs:

> Koran 8:12 *Then your Lord spoke to His angels and said, "I will be with you. Give strength to the believers. I will send terror into the kafirs' hearts, cut off their heads and even the tips of their fingers!"*

All of Western logic is based upon the law of contradiction—if two things contradict, then at least one of them is false. But Islamic logic is dualistic; two things can contradict each other and both are true.

No dualistic system may be measured by one answer. This is the reason that the arguments about what constitutes the "real" Islam go on and on and are never resolved. A single right answer does not exist.

Dualistic systems can only be measured by statistics. It is futile to argue that one side of the dualism is true. For an example of using statistics, look at the question: what is the real jihad, the jihad of inner, spiritual struggle or the jihad of war? Let's turn to Bukhari (the Hadith) for the answer, as he repeatedly speaks of jihad. In Bukhari, 97% of the references to jihad are about war and 3% are about the inner struggle. So the statistical answer is that jihad is 97% war and 3% inner struggle. Is jihad war? Yes—97%. Is jihad inner struggle? Yes—3%. So if you are writing an article, you can make a case for either. But in truth, almost every argument about Islam can be answered by "all of the above." Both sides of the duality are right.

What is the real Islam? Is it the religion of peace or is it the jihad of killing? The correct answer is both. Islam is dualistic. Therefore, Islam is peace and Islam is violence. The violence cannot be removed or reformed. If the basis of violence is removed, then what is left is not Islam. If the submission and duality are removed, then what is left is not Islam.

THE TWO CIVILIZATIONS

There are only two types of ethics—unitary and dualistic. Unitary ethics are based upon the Golden Rule. The Golden Rule has no limits as to whom to treat as ourselves. That is, the Golden Rule sees all of the world as one body.

For instance, "Do unto some others (or your friends or tribe members) as you would have them do unto you" is not the Golden Rule. No, the Golden Rule is "Do unto others (each and every human)" and the others had no qualifications. All humans are seen as one body to be treated fairly.

The other ethical system is dualistic, like Islamic ethics.

What is important is to see that Christianity, Buddhism, Judaism, Hinduism, and most atheists agree on the Golden Rule. This ethical basis is so important that we can see that all of the groups share a common unitary civilization that is based upon our very humanity and the Golden Rule.

But Islam has no part in a unitary civilization. Islam is a dualistic civilization that divides all of humanity into believers and kafirs. There is no humanity, as such. Kafirs and believers are to be treated differently. And, even worse, Islam declares that its fundamental purpose is to annihilate the unitary civilization. The dualistic civilization is based upon submission and duality. It cannot be reformed or changed.

THE POVERTY OF ISLAM

Only the land of Islam—dar al Islam—is real to a Muslim. As an example of how self-centered Islam is, only 210 books per year[1] are translated into Arabic—the same number of books translated into Lithuanian. There has never been a best selling novel that has been translated into Arabic. Why are so few books translated? From an Islamic standpoint, the books are not needed. They are not Islam; they are not necessary. The books have no real knowledge in them.

Not one Nobel Prize in the sciences has been awarded to anyone in the Islamic world—eight prizes have been awarded to Muslim scientists who worked in the West with Western partners. Their work took place outside Islamic culture. For perspective, look at how many prizes have been awarded to tiny Scotland: 32.

The total economic output (not counting oil revenues) of the Arabic world equals that of Finland. The extreme poverty of Islamic economics must be explained. Mohammed's sacred economic example was to violently take the non-Muslim's wealth. Mohammed did not create wealth. He took it.

Dual ethics leads to a culture of slyness and deceit that hurts business. Once you can treat the "other" badly, you have learned how to treat your brother badly.

The Koranic doctrine leads to fatalism—a poor business principle. Fatalism is the opposite of creativity, initiative and hard work.

It is not generally recognized, but the Taliban of Afghanistan is a reform movement (remember that the next time someone says that Islam just needs a reformation). One of the results of its success was the destruction of cities and the killing of Muslims. Indeed, the biggest killer of Muslims is Islam.

QUESTIONS

Islam makes many demands upon the kafirs. How does that statement illustrate both submission and duality?

---

1. According to UNESCO's Index Translationum (www.unesco.org/culture/xtrans/), only 6,881 books (mostly technical works) have been translated into Arabic since 1970. From the days of the Ottoman Empire (about 500 years) there have been about 100,000 books translated into Arabic. This is the number translated into Greek each year.

Is there anything you have read about Islam in this study guide that is not about submission or duality?

Can you name a single great work of art, music or literature that is Islamic? One answer is poetry, such as that by Rumi. The other answer is calligraphy. Otherwise, it is an Islamic desert in art.

If it were not for the oil, what would be the economic status of the Arab world?

"Islam is the religion of peace." Why does the media say that? Name six things that contradict that statement.

How does dualism and submission make for bad business?

Dualism means that any statement by a Muslim about Islam is probably half true, but it also means that it is half false. Discuss. Can you give any examples?

SMYRNA

Lesson 12

SUMMARY

- Jihad has killed over 60,000,000 Christians. The destruction of the Christians in Smyrna is told here.

- Islam attacked the Christians of Smyrna in 1922. It was an annihilation that took place as the Christian Europeans stood aside.

Before jihad exploded out of Arabia, Turkey (Asia Minor) was a Christian nation of primarily Greek culture called Anatolia. Today Turkey is 99.7% Islamic and increasing. How did this happen?

Islam tried for centuries to crush Christianity and the Greek culture in Turkey. Constantinople, the capital, fell to jihad in 1453. Christians became dhimmis, second-class citizens. The slow grind of discrimination was punctuated by outbursts of violence. Christian Greek Anatolia was painfully changed into Islamic Turkey.

The background for these stories is that in World War I Turkey sided with the Germans (Islam sided with the Nazis in WWII). In this political chaos, Kamal Attaturk rose to power as head of the military and political government. The Allies were exhausted and did not want to get involved with another war, so they gave money to support the Greeks to fight the Turks. Long story made short, the Greeks lost.

The old Ottoman empire had fallen and a new government was arising. The leader, Attaturk, was determined to destroy the last of the kafirs in Turkey. But what he talked about to the Westerners was the possibility of business in a new country. World War I was over and America was becoming a world power. America wanted trade and influence.

The war had brought about new technology and a fusion between industry and government. A concept called Dollar Diplomacy was practiced. Trade and diplomacy became two ends of the same stick. To show how far this concept went, the American ambassador took the funds that had been raised by Christians to help the Armenians persecuted in northern Turkey and gave it to the Turks. When the Christians protested to the media, the media would not report it because of State department pressure.

The Muslim Turks killed both Greeks and Armenians that day, but this lesson will focus on the murder and theft of the Armenians. Armenia was one of the first Christian nations and has suffered monstrously at the hands of Islam. Armenia was well educated and prosperous and had always been especially despised by Islam.

Over a million Armenians were killed in Turkey in the 20th century.

There are two forms of evil in this story. The first evil is what was done by jihad. The second evil was what was *not* done by the dhimmi kafirs. As you read this story of the destruction of Smyrna, know that this same story is repeated today by the same players and with the same results.

IT STARTS

Smyrna was in what was once called Asia Minor, also Anatolia. It was one of the oldest communities of Christians left in Turkey. Islam had already destroyed the other six.

> Revelation 1:11 *saying, "What you see, write in a book and send to the seven assemblies: to Ephesus, Smyrna, Pergamum, Thyatira, Sardis, Philadelphia, and to Laodicea."*

Smyrna, Turkey, in 1922 was a dazzling city. It was a fusion of Christian, Armenian, Greek, and Mediterranean, with some Muslims. (It was like Beirut, Lebanon, before it fell to jihad. All multicultural politics that includes Islam will fall to Islam. There have never been any exceptions.)

The West had given the Greeks the responsibility of containing the Turkish army and then turned around and prevented its victory by interference. Now the Turks, lead by Attaturk [a Muslim military leader who became ruler], began to enter the city.

The Armenians were afraid. They had experienced Islam in their old homeland in northern Turkey where the Turkish genocide had killed their ancestors. There were many warships from England, America, France and Italy in the harbor. Large numbers of commercial freighters were there from every country. The Armenians began to crowd down to the harbor. None of the freighters would take them on. They, along with the Allied warships in the harbor, were declared to be neutral and did not want to interfere with the politics of the rising Turkish power. They were in Smyrna for business and refugees were political. Other Armenians were unafraid; they believed that the warships from Christian nations would protect them.

The Turkish army entered Smyrna and began to loot the shops of the Greeks and the Armenians. Then the army turned from looting to armed robbery. Then the Turks began to rob and kill the Armenians.

Aboard the American ship *Litchfield*, Captain Hepburn wrote that the Turks deserved high marks for discipline and high military standards. The cover-up had started.

The Turkish army surrounded the Armenian quarter and all Muslims were told to leave the area.

KILLING THE CHRISTIAN LEADER

Chrysostomos was the leader of the Orthodox Christians and went to see the local commanding officer to try to arrange the evacuation of Christians. He approached the general and extended his hand. The general spit on him. He pushed Chrysostomos out the door and yelled at the Muslim crowd, "Treat him as he deserves."

The crowd dragged him down the street until they reached a barbershop. Chrysostomos needed a shave the crowd decided. They pulled his beard out and rubbed dog excrement on him. The man with the straight razor cut off an ear and, at the sight of blood, the mob went mad trying to get close to Chrysostomos, who was barely able to murmur, "Receive my soul into Thy Kingdom, O Lord," before he died. They cut out his eyes, ears and nose.

There were French marines standing by and their officer forbade them to defend the Christian. The body was dragged further down the street, when they stopped and cut off his privates and put them in his dead mouth.

When they reported his murder to the French Admiral Dumesnil, he said, "He got what was coming to him."

NOWHERE TO RUN

In the harbor small boats carried refugees to the ships. No one would let them come aboard. When people jumped into the water and clutched the lines, the sailors cut the lines and poured boiling water on the people. They would not break their "neutrality".

Turkish forces now moved house to house in the Armenian quarter. They broke down the doors and robbed the men. The Muslim men brutally violated the women and then pushed them naked into the streets. Men were tied together to be marched outside the city and killed. Orders went out to use the sword and stop shooting the men. The guns were too noisy, and at the time, the Turks insisted nothing was happening. As many as a hundred men were lashed at the wrists and beheaded.

Lieutenant Merrill, an American, wrote to Admiral Bristol (the top American official in Turkey) that, "No one could imagine without seeing them under fire what a chicken-livered lot the Christian minorities (Greek and Armenian) are."[1]

Major Davis of the Red Cross cabled Admiral Bristol that the refugees must be evacuated. The Turks were going to solve their "race" problem by annihilation.

The American consul was exhausted. He was constantly besieged by Armenians who told the same story of murder and theft. Captain Hepburn sent for the Turkish army to drive them away from the Consulate. Later that day, he boarded the *Litchfield*. He sat and watched as two newsmen typed up their reports. One of them stopped and read what he had written. He threw it into the wastebasket and said he could not send it in. It would ruin his ability to report in Turkey after this was over. The other reporter agreed that they should dig up some old stories how the Greek Orthodox Christian soldiers had committed wrongs against the Turks.

They were desperate for something to offset the evil of jihad. And they did. The news wires were filled with reports of Greeks and Armenians looting before the Turkish troops arrived. They emphasized the discipline of the Turkish troops.

But not everyone lied:

> 'The Armenian quarter is a charnel house[2],' a French officer noted on 13 September: 'In three days this rich quarter is entirely ravaged. The streets are heaped with mattresses, broken furniture, glass, torn paintings. Some young women and girls, especially pretty ones, have been taken away and put into a house that is guarded by [Muslim] Turkish sentries. They must submit to the whims of the patrols. One sees cadavers in front of the houses. They are swollen and some have exposed entrails. The smell is unbearable and swarms of flies cover them. Day and night I make a tour of this quarter, and women who are crazed join me in the street; their clothes torn, their hair flying wild, they attach themselves to me. They beg me to take them from this quarter. First there are four, then eight, then a dozen and the number of women grows. I am in uniform and just about the only one to circulate on foot. Where to take them? Everywhere is filled:

---

1 Smyrna, 1922, M H Dobkin, Newmark Press, NY, NY, 1989, pg. 136.
2 A charnel house is a place where bodies are deposited.

the churches, the schools, the Alliance Francaise are overflowing. So I disengage myself and try to reassure them. There are no men in this quarter; all are dead, or hiding, or they have been taken away.[1]

The *New York Times* reported that Attaturk was punishing any soldier who violated his orders to respect life and property.

BUSINESS IS BUSINESS

In Constantinople Admiral Chester and his two sons saw that a lifetime dream was to be fulfilled. His Ottoman-American Development Company would obtain a 99-year contract to all the sand and gravel for road building and all right-of-way needed from quarries. All imports would be exempt from duties and taxes.

He had written in *Current History* that the Turks had been falsely accused during the World War. They had been benevolent to the Armenians and other minorities.

Admiral Bristol was encouraging American businessmen to get in on the deals before the Europeans got the contracts.

NOW THE FIRE

The Turks now started to bring in kerosene. Sacks of "food" turned out to be gunpowder and dynamite. Wagons filled with barrels of gasoline were brought in.

The winds shifted away from the Muslim quarter and the fires started. As the firemen would be trying to put out the fires in one house, the Muslims were pouring gasoline in the next house.

'In all the houses I went into I saw dead bodies,' Tchorbadjis [a French officer] said. 'In one house I followed a trail of blood that led me to a cupboard. My curiosity forced me to open this cupboard—and my hair stood on end. Inside was the naked body of a girl, with her front cut off. At another house there was a girl hanging from a lemon tree in the yard. There were plenty of armed soldiers going about. One of them went in where there was an Armenian family hiding and massacred the lot. When he came out his scimitar was dripping with blood. He cleaned it on his boots and leggings.

'On one of the roads I saw a man about forty-five or fifty years old. The Turks had blinded him and cut off his nose and left him on the streets. He

---

[1]   Ibid, pg. 150.

was crying out, in Turkish, "Isn't there anyone here Christian enough to shoot me so that I will not get burnt in the fire ?"[2]

In the end, the entire Armenian quarter was burned. Some of the survivors were able to be evacuated.

WRAPPING UP THE NEWS

Admiral Bristol's biggest headache of the moment was the press. Eyewitnesses arriving at foreign ports were already giving out spectacular news stories to reporters, and it seemed inevitable that after the mass exodus there would be a barrage of uncontrollable publicity. On 22 September the Admiral had cabled the State Department urging the release of an official account to offset 'exaggerated and alarming reports appearing in American newspapers regarding Smyrna fires'. He offered a sample which the State Department was pleased to use:

> American officers who have been eyewitnesses of all events occurring, Smyrna, from time of the occupation of that city by Nationalists up to present, report killings which occurred at that city were ones for the most part by individuals or small bands of rowdies or soldiers, and that nothing in the nature of a massacre had occurred. During the fire some people were drowned by attempting to swim to vessels in harbor or by falling off the quay wall, but this number was small. When masses of people were gathered on quay to escape fire, they were guarded by Turkish troops but were at no time prevented by such troops from leaving the quay if they so desired. It is impossible to estimate the number of deaths due to killings, fire, and execution, but the total probably does not exceed 2,000.

Bristol's tone suited the policy makers. In the next issue of *Foreign Affairs* Elihu Root, (Secretary of State) was pleading for "restraint of expression", noting that "nations are even more sensitive to insult than individuals".[3]

As far as the estimate that 2,000 died, 190,000 Armenians were never accounted for.

CHRISTIAN MARTYRS

The deaths alone are a tragedy, but the supreme tragedy is that they have all died in vain. Every Christian knows about the number of Jews killed by Hitler, but what Christian knows about the deaths of their own?

---

2 Ibid, 157
3 Ibid, pgs. 200-201.

Why did the Muslims do this? It was a sacred act. It is strictly according to the code of jihad that is laid out in the Koran and the Sunna [see the Ethics chapter]. Indeed, murder and theft of the kafir in jihad is a sacrament. If one of the Muslim jihadists had been killed, he would be declared a martyr.

The sword of the jihadist is the scalpel of Allah; it is pure good. Just as a scalpel removes what harms the body, jihad, in all its forms, removes what is offensive to Allah. The Muslims who did these acts were "good and moderate" Muslims. Mohammed did these things and he defines moderation and righteous action. A jihadist is a Mohammedan.

The great stain on Christianity is that those who sought to follow Christ suffered death and destruction under jihad and they had no support of the Christian community.

When a mosque is even chipped by a kafir every Muslim roars in unity. When the Muslims desecrated the church in Bethlehem in the late 20th century, the silence of Christians was deafening.

THE FINAL LESSON

The mind of those who aided Islam in Smyrna by ignoring the suffering of the victims of jihad is dhimmitude. Yes, they were greedy, but they also did not have any any knowledge about the doctrine and history of political Islam. The businessmen, diplomats, and military men were clueless about the real evil happening and how it was just the next step to further suffering.

It is not that Islam is so strong, but that kafirs are so weak. Ignorance of the doctrine and history of political Islam blinds the kafirs.

Today, the Armenians are trying to tell their story, but no one cares, no one listens. Turkey denies the annihilation and is trying to become a part of the European Union. No one wants to talk about what could be bad for business, so the EU does not want to talk about it. It upsets the Muslims.

In the 20th century, America went to war to support the Muslims in Kosovo, Yugoslavia and Albania. The press and State department played the same roles there as they did in Smyrna. The supreme tragedy is that Christians in America played the same role that they did in 1922. We have no knowledge about the suffering of kafirs over the centuries. If we are to survive as a civilization, we must study Islam. It is not that Islam is so strong: it is that our ignorance makes us weak.

The Armenians are only a small part of the Tears of Jihad[1]. What happened to the Hindus in India was exactly like this. Political Islam is remarkably steadfast over the centuries and geography. This is because every action and thought is driven by the doctrine found in the Trilogy. Kafirs always think that Islam will change. Islam does not change because it cannot change and it does not need to change. The same doctrine keeps winning, so there is no need to change.

If Christians do not learn the doctrine and history of political Islam, then one day in Ameristan, some Muslim will say to another, "Did you know that there used to be many churches here back when it was called America?" And the other Muslim will say, "I saw one in a picture once."

Lebanon was a Christian nation in 1960. Today they are a shrinking minority.

Christians like to draw distinctions among themselves. But Islam draws absolutely no distinction between Protestant, Evangelical, Catholic, Orthodox… Jihad destroyed each and every one.

Islam is right on this issue. All religions (except Islam) unite in the belief about the Golden Rule. It is this common ethical, cultural, political system that is based upon the Golden Rule that violates the Islamic civilization of submission and duality. Christianity must be destroyed for Islam to exist. In the end there is no co-existence now, then or in the future.

The philosophy of turning the other cheek to Mohammed has failed for 1400 years. The philosophy of ignorance has failed for 1400 years. It is failing today and it will fail tomorrow. Christians must learn and act or cease to exist. That is as certain as a falling apple will hit the ground.

QUESTIONS

How do you feel about not knowing this story?

What do you think the stories about the other six churches mentioned in Revelation are like?

Was the violation of women a sin from the standpoint of Islam?

Was it Sunna to kill Chrysostomos?

---

1   The Tears of Jihad refers to the 270,000,000 killed in jihad over the last 1400 years.

The European and American Christians stood by. How do we see the same thing today?

Were the jihadists moderate or extremist Muslims?

What is there in Christians that makes them deny the suffering of Christians at the hands of Islam? [As you look for answers, know that Jews, Buddhists, intellectuals and Hindus do the same thing about their own victims of jihad.]

Do you have any understanding about why Christians are 3% of Iraq's population, but form 30% of Iraq's immigrants?

In light of Islamic ethics, what was unethical about the annihilation of Christianity in Smyrna?

All of the information in this lesson was adapted from *Smyrna, 1922* by M H Dobkin, Newmark Press, NY, NY, 1989. This story here is only the smallest part of the suffering of the Armenians.

CONCLUSION

SUMMARY

- We must learn and use the right names and words for Islam. Wrong names make for wrong thinking.

- Without the oil, Islam is poor in wealth, art, writing, education and every other measure of success.

- Islam excels at only one thing—war, jihad. Once Islam enters a culture, it will ultimately eliminate every detail of its existence.

- Islam is here to Islamicize our civilization. For 1400 years the kafirs have denied the existence of Islamic politics and denied a suffering under jihad, dhimmitude and slavery.

- If we are to save our civilization, we must know Islam for what it is. We must know that we will lose all we hold dear if we don't engage our self-declared enemy in a war of survival.

NAMES

All of the names and terms used by Islam come from the Trilogy, but kafirs don't use these terms or names.

The jihad of Umar burst out of Arabia and crushed the Christian world of Syria, Egypt, and the rest of the Middle East. The Christians recorded it as an Arabic war. When Islam invaded Europe, Europeans called it a Turkish invasion. The jihad against Christian Spain was an invasion by the Moors. The Muslims called these events jihad.

In the early nineteenth century America sent the Navy and Marines to war against the Barbary pirates in North Africa. But the Muslims never called their naval raiders "Barbary pirates." They called them *ghazis,* sacred raiders. Naming them pirates showed that the kafirs had no idea about the doctrine and history of Islam.

Look at the news today. The media report an *intifada*, an uprising, by the Palestinians against the Israelis. But the terms *intifada, Palestinian,* and *Israeli* are misnomers. The truer terms are *jihad, Muslim,* and *kafir.* The doctrine of political Islam clearly states that jihad is to be waged by all

Muslims against all Jews and other kafirs. Today is no different from 1,400 years ago in Islam.

The events of 9/11 are recorded in the West as an attack by terrorists. Mohammed Atta, the leader of the 9/11 attack, was a pious Muslim. He left a letter clearly stating his intentions: 9/11 was pure jihad. A terror attack is a tactic, but jihad is a 1,400-year continuous process. Therefore, a terrorist attack is not the same as jihad.

The "War on Terror" is a bogus phrase that is useless since it does nothing to define the enemy. The proper phrase is "War against Political Islam".

The words "radical" Muslim and "good" Muslim are used in the media. The word "radical" does not appear anywhere in the Trilogy. A "good" Muslim is defined in the Trilogy as a Muslim who follows the Sunna. Osama bin Laden is a good Muslim since he follows the Koran of Medina. When the media uses the phrase "good" Muslim, they mean a Muslim they are not afraid of, a Muslim who follows the Koran of Mecca.

Keep in mind that all Muslims accept the authority of the Koran, Sira and Hadith in their entirety. When they speak with you, you never get the whole truth, just part of it.

Muslims' terms for their actions connect events and people with Islamic history and doctrine and show a continuing process. Non-Muslim terms are misnomers, do not connect events, and show no meaning of historic process.

The only correct terms are those of Islam. The naming by the kafirs is wrong because the naming is a projection of Western culture. Correct naming comes from Islam and leads to correct thinking.

THE SUPREME MASTER OF CIVILIZATIONAL WAR

Mohammed was the supreme master of complete war and has had no equal to this day. His understanding of the use of force was sophisticated and subtle. Physical violence was only a small part of his understanding of war. That is why comparisons make him superior to military men such as Julius Caesar. Other military geniuses established empires, but none of them had a process for war and empire that lasted for fourteen-hundred years and is still going strong.

Mohammed's profound insight was not only the waging of physical war but also war of the mind, emotions, culture, politics, and religion. There is no aspect of being human that Mohammed did not use for war. Money, salvation, treatment of women, culture, religion, destiny, family, immigration, legal codes, government, power, slavery, deceit, racial pride, tribalism, community, fear, propaganda, diplomacy, spy-craft, philosophy, ethics, and psychology were all used for jihad. Jihad is complete and total civilizational war.

CIVILIZATIONAL WAR

Today we refer to cultures on the basis of continents, but up until 600 AD, the cultural reference was oriented to the Mediterranean Sea. Egypt was only a few days away from Italy, and Greek ships sailed into Egyptian harbors on a regular basis. Egypt and North Africa were much closer to the European culture than African culture south of the Sahara. There was a Buddhist monastery in Alexandria, Egypt. The southern coast of the Mediterranean was Roman, then became Christian. St. Augustine was from what is now called North Africa. Turkey was Buddhist and Christian. Iran (Persia) was Zoroastrian. The Hindu culture covered an area twice as large as it is now.

More than half of Christianity disappeared, half of Hindu culture disappeared, half of Buddhism was annihilated, Zoroasterism disappeared, and languages disappeared to be replaced by Arabic. The laws, customs, names, and history became extinct. When Napoleon invaded Egypt, he found that the Egyptian Muslims did not know anything about the pyramids or temples. Islam had annihilated the memory of a 5,000-year-old Coptic Egyptian culture. The culture of the Pharaohs was not even a memory. Our knowledge of ancient Egypt did not come from the Muslims, but from our archeology.

Islam annihilates all cultures over time. Turkey used to be a wonderful Greek culture, Anatolia. North Africa was home to the now vanishing native North African Berber culture. The dualistic civilization of Islam annihilates all other cultures.

Bagdad was home to the oldest community of Jews in the world. They came there during the Babylonian captivity. Today there are fewer than two dozen Jews left in Iraq. When they die, the last trace of an ancient Jewish culture will disappear. Islam annihilates all cultures that live within its borders over a period of time. They eventually either leave or convert. There are no exceptions.

There has been no other form of war that has produced permanent government. Once jihad has conquered a civilization, it never has another revolution. There has never been a revolution against Islamic government. The form of government may change, but it stays Islam. The only time that Islam has left any government has been by outside force. Spain and Eastern Europe were freed of Islam only by outside help.

ISLAMIZATION OF A CULTURE

The Sira gives a dynamic picture of how Islam enters a culture. When Mohammed started preaching in Mecca, he did not encounter animosity. Islam was portrayed as a logical continuation of the native Arabic religions. Then Islam claimed to be a "brother religion" to Judaism. Next it became not just a better religion but the best, and all of the other religions were wrong. Islam was publicly confrontational, attacking every aspect of the host culture. Hostility developed between Islam and the Meccan culture of religious tolerance. The Meccans tried to placate the Muslims, but there could be no compromise. Islam turned increasingly to violence that culminated in a treaty of war with new allies in Medina.

When the Muslims immigrated to Medina, the Immigrants[1] were peaceful. But when the Jews said that Mohammed was not a prophet in the Jewish tradition, Islam became hostile. Islam was the better religion;,and if logic did not show that, then forceful arguments would. Up to this point, the process of Islam in Medina was the same as in Mecca.

The Immigrants were very poor and there was little growth of the religion. In Medina Mohammed found a way to obtain money and settle old scores with the Meccans who had never submitted to Islam. The solution was political—jihad against the Meccans, the Jews, and their neighbors. By jihad, political Islam conquered all of Arabia in nine years. [Mohammed was in Medina for 10 years; jihad occupied the last 9 years.]

Islam is here now to take part in our freedom and equality. But Islam is here to destroy freedom and replace it with the slavery of Allah. Muslims in Europe are already demanding that they be judged by Sharia law. The long term goals of all Mohammedans is to replace all governments with Sharia law.

WHAT YOU STILL DON'T KNOW

These *Thirteen Lessons* have given you a start on Islam. What you don't know is the actual history of Islam. The killing of 270,000,000 people by jihad is a hidden history that is not taught in any school.

Liberals always bring up the Crusades as a black mark against Christianity. And for sure, European Christians did some very wrong things, like attacking other Christians and Jews. But the main thrust of the Crusades was that it was one of three times that Christian civilization responded to

---

1   The Immigrant is a sacred figure in Islam. The term is Answar in Arabic. Mohammed was an Immigrant when he moved from Mecca to Medina.

Islamic terror. Robert Spencer's book, *The Politically Incorrect Guide to the Crusades,* is a must read.

One of the sad things is when Christians decide to try to do something about Islam, they repeat 1400 years of mistakes.

One of these mistakes is to assume that the Gospels will convert Muslims and that religion is the key to resisting Islam. When Christians talk about Jesus and the New Testament, they are carrying water from a poisoned well from the Muslim's point of view. Every Muslim believes that the New Testament is corrupt and the real Jesus is Isa of the Koran. The Christians' Jesus is not the real Jesus to a Muslim.

A Muslim will say that they accept Jesus as one of their prophets and that Abraham is their ancestor and prophet.

Politics and Mohammed are the key to attacking Islam. The average Muslim is remarkably ignorant about Mohammed and Islam's true history. The truth of Mohammed and the deaths of 270 million are the key to dealing with a Muslim.

So the first step in converting a Muslim is to first convert him to apostasy (leaving Islam). And how do you do that? Forget about the Koran and Allah. Teach a Muslim about Mohammed. A Christian knows about Christ, but a Muslim knows virtually nothing about Mohammed. Teach a Muslim about slavery, the assassinations, the killing of the Jews, jihad and the rest of the material here. You will be amazed about how little they know about Mohammed.

When you attack Islam by saying Muslims are terrorists, they reply that America and Israel are the terrorists. If you criticize the treatment of women, they reply that they honor and respect women. When you speak of Mohammed, they can make no denial. Mohammed is both the strength and the Achilles heel of Islam.

Attack the the material and intellectual poverty of Islamic civilization. Don't just preach salvation, talk politics. Remember, religion is the least part of Islam. Mohammed is the key to conversion.

IGNORANCE

Why don't Christian schools teach about the doctrine and history of Islam? Are Christians fearful that if their children learn about Islam, they will convert? Islam is here today. Islam is here for one purpose—to Islamicize the kafirs. Turkey and the Middle East were Christian until Islam entered. Why are we pretending that 1400 years of history of Christian persecution won't continue?

There is no Christian school that teaches the doctrine of Islam based upon the Trilogy or the history of suffering of the Christians under Islam. How can this be justified?

Why don't Christians know the real story of the Crusades? Muslims and Leftists taunt Christians about the Crusades. Learn the true story of the Crusades.

To give you a measure of our ignorance, now that you have finished this 13 lesson study you know much, much more about political Islam than any Senator, Congressman, governor, rabbi or 99.9% of all preachers, professors or media reporters.

SAVING OUR CIVILIZATION

We do not want our civilization to fall because we are ignorant. When the transmission goes out on your car, you don't pray over it. You go to a transmission shop. For 1400 years Christians have believed that Jesus could beat Allah. It has not worked for 1400 years; why would it work now?

Oh yes, we all know a story of how someone managed to convert a Muslim to Christ, but while that one Muslim left Islam, a thousand more were born into it. Odds of a 1000 to 1 are not winning odds. If Christians do not wake up, America will be like Turkey, 99.7% Muslim and 0.3% Christian and falling. Now those are thin odds.

You probably don't understand how the automatic transmission in your car works, but that is not an ethical concern. Is it ethical to turn a blind eye towards something that will destroy your community, nation, civilization and your church? How can any Christian justify ignorance about what can destroy the church?

Imagine that you have to give a talk to high school aged Christians. How would you write a talk to convince them that they should not learn about the history and doctrine of Islam? What would you give as the advantages of ignorance?

Imagine if Christian colleges had every graduate schooled in the basics of Islam and its history. Even one course would be a vast improvement. The rest of the world is ignorant of Islam. Imagine how powerfully influential they would be. Imagine how they could help save our civilization.

There have some small changes, but there must be large changes in how Christians teach about Islam. Now that you have read this study, you can see that there need not be any fear of a Christian studying this material and converting to Islam.

WORK TO BE DONE

The first step is to realize the danger of annihilation and extinction. The second step is to realize that our present course of having our heads in the sand or being too polite to bring up a distasteful subject will lead to our annihilation as a civilization.

The third step is to realize that Christianity must survive. To survive, churches must realize that it has been war for 1400 years in Europe, Asia and Africa and that the war is here in America today and will not cease.

The black churches are the beachhead of Islam in America. Islam is telling black Americans that Christianity is the "white man's" religion and that Islam is the natural religion of the black man. Islamic proselytizing is a fire storm in the prisons. Christians must be able to take the story of Islamic enslavement of Africa into black America.

The last thing for Christians to realize is that they are the only hope of saving our civilization. Our politicians have already sold out to Islam. They will listen to no criticism of Islam and only want the Muslim vote. Universities have declared Islam to be the new "minority" to be curried and favored. The media are ignorant. Secular humanists resist Islam, but only as individuals.

Christians are the only enemies of Islam that are organized. The organization is the only way to oppose another organization. You can't run Walmart out of business with a yard sale held out of the back of a pickup truck.

If Christians do for the next 1400 years what they have done for the last 1400 years, there will not be a single Christian left, not even in the history books. When you open a history book in Pakistan, there is no trace of Hinduism (Pakistan was part of Hindustan). Pakistani history does not even start until Islam invaded. If we do not defeat Islam, in the year 3007 AH (after Haj), the history books will not show any sign of the USA or Christianity, just Ameristan.

In the face of Islam, Christians have been lambs led to the slaughter. The tragedy is that the slaughtered lambs have been forgotten.

Christianity has one vast advantage in this war and that is the true doctrine and history of Islam. But that weapon is useless until Christians become masters of that knowledge. The sword of truth is useful only when you know the truth.

One last word. If you think that Islam is bad now, wait until the oil starts running out in 30 years. Without the oil, the economic output of the entire Arabic culture is less than that of Finland. Millions upon millions of impoverished, starving Muslims will push into Europe and America.

Immigration is the first step of jihad. Think about Medina. Think about Eurabia and Ameristan. Today, in England, there are more Muslims in the mosques on Friday than there are Christians in church on Sunday.

QUESTIONS

Why is it not possible to think clearly without the right words?

Since there is never a news report that uses Islamic words as names, what does that say about the quality of the report?

Christians usually think of themselves as being a member of a religion. If you are trying to convert a Muslim, how does that make you limited in effectiveness?

How is jihad a civilizational war?

Why are Christians afraid to talk about Islam?

Why don't' Christian schools teach about the doctrine and history of Islam?

Mohammed said that Christians are endlessly divided. True? False? How does this division help Islam?

What are reasons for hope in resisting Islam? What are reasons for despair?

READING LIST

DOCTRINE—THE SUNNA

Sira—the life of Mohammed.

Mohammed and the Unbelievers, Center for the Study of Political Islam, 2006.

Spencer, Robert. *The Truth about Muhammad*. Regnery Publishing, 2006.

The definitive work:

Guillaume, A. *The Life of Muhammad*, (Ishaq's—*Sirat Rasul Allah*). Karachi: Oxford University Press, 1967.

HADITH—THE TRADITIONS OF MOHAMMED

The Political Traditions of Mohammed, Center for the Study of Political Islam, 2006.

The Hadith of Abu Al-Bukhari, Sahih Bukhari is best found on the internet. The University of Southern California (http://www.usc.edu/dept/MSA/fundamentals/hadithsunnah/) is one of the best sites.

DOCTRINE—THE KORAN

A Simple Koran, Center for the Study of Political Islam, 2006.

An Abridged Koran, Center for the Study of Political Islam, 2006.

HISTORY OF JIHAD

Bostom, Andrew. *The Legacy of Jihad*. Prometheus Books, 2006.

GOOD PRIMER

Davis, Greg. *Religion of Peace?* World Ahead Publishing, Los Angels, CA.

BEST ONE BOOK SOURCE

Warraq, Ibn. *Why I Am Not a Muslim*. Prometheus Books, 1999.

DHIMMITUDE

Ye'or, Bat. *The Dhimmi*. Associated University Presses, Cranbury, NJ, 2003.

WEB SITES

The Web is an excellent place to learn about Islam. Here are some of the current best sites.

www.jihadwatch.org Robert Spencer posts articles about Islam, jihad and dhimmitude

www.frontpagemag.com David Horowitz posts news articles including many about Islam and jihad.

www.gatesofvienna.blogspot.com commentary on political news and Islam by Christian husband and wife

www.faithfreedom.org Ali Sina, a Shia Muslim apostate posts original articles, news about Islam

www.littlegreenfootballs.com/weblog political news, Islam and jihad news from all over the world

www.americansagainsthate.org Joe Kaufman posts news, articles, commentary on Islam and jihad

www.memri.org The Middle East Media Research Institute translates Islam news and tv shows

www.danielpipes.org Noted mid-east and Islamic scholar Daniel Pipes excellent web site

www.peoplestruthforum.com Jeffrey Epstein's excellent Terrorism Update

www.americancongressfortruth.com Brigitte Gabriel's web site

www.counterterrorism.org Articles by many terrorism experts such as Steve Emerson

www.westernresistance.com (Europe) Excellent update on jihad around the world.

www.librabunda.blogspot.com Mark Alexander, a Christian from Britain, writes about jihad and Islam.

www.brusselsjournal.com (Belgium) The voice of Christian conservative politics and jihad in Europe.

www.siteinstitute.org Rita Katz excellent site, Search for International Terrorist Entities.

www.islam-watch.org/index.html Islam scrutinized by ex-Muslims

www.americastruthforum.com comprehensive new about jihad from around the world

http://islamthreat.blogspot.com Christian Middle Eastern Americans Council

GLOSSARY

When you learn new words you can think new thoughts. Islam is based on concepts that are totally foreign to us and to understand Islam, you need new words.

ablution, a ritual washing to become clean for religious acts.

abrogation, the Koran is filled with verses that contradict each other. The doctrine of abrogation is that the verse that is written later is better that the earlier verse.

Abu Bakr, Mohammed's closet companion and his father-in-law, the first caliph.

Abu Talib, Mohammed's uncle, who adopted him, taught him how to be a caravan trader, and protected him in his role as a tribal elder. He died a kafir and was condemned to Hell by Mohammed.

ahadith, the Arabic plural of hadith; hadiths is used in English.

Aisha, Mohammed's favorite wife of the harem. He married her at six and consummated the marriage at age nine. She was eighteen when he died. Many of the hadiths are from her.

Ali, Mohammed's cousin and son-in-law. He is considered the head of the Shia sect and was the fourth caliph (the first caliph, according the Shias).

Ansars, the Helpers. The Ansars were the first converts in Medina and gave money and shelter to the Muslims who left Mecca to come with Mohammed.

apostate, one who has left a religion, in particular, Islam. The Koran says that apostasy is the worst sin possible. It is far worse than mass murder. Mohammed and Abu Bakr killed apostates.

Black Stone, a dark stone, roughly seven inches in diameter. It is set into the corner of the Kabah. It was there before Mohammed.

caliph, a political and religious leader of Islam, roughly a pope-king.

circumambulate, to move in a circle around the Kabah while praying.

companion, one who knew Mohammed.

Copt, Copts were the original Egyptians, their ancestors included the pharaohs.

dhimmi, a kafir who is "protected" by Islam. A dhimmi has no civil rights, for instance, cannot testify in courts against a Muslim. Today, a dhimmi is a kafir who defers to Islam, an apologist for Islam.

Five Pillars of Islam, praying five times a day; paying the zakat, the Islamic tax; fasting during Ramadan, going on pilgrimage to Mecca; and declaring that there is no god, but Allah and Mohammed is his prophet.

Gabriel, an archangel of Allah, who relayed the Koran to Mohammed.

ghira, absolute control of a woman's sexuality in all of its forms is part of a man's ghira (pride, honor, self-respect and sacred jealousy).

hadith, a Tradition, or small story, about what Mohammed said and did.

Hadith, a collection of hadiths.

haj, (hajj), the pilgrimage to Mecca.

Helpers, the first Muslim converts of Medina who helped the Muslims who came from Mecca, known as the Ansar in Arabic.

Holy Spirit, the archangel, Gabriel, in Islam.

Hudaybiya, an area near Mecca. It is famous because Mohammed was recognized as a political leader when he signed a treaty. It is important to kafirs because Mohammed showed that Islam only enters into treaties when weak and will break them when it becomes strong.

imam, an Islamic religious leader of the Sunni sect.

immigrants, those who left Mecca with Mohammed.

isnad, the chain of witnesses who relayed a hadith. The source person must have personally heard and saw what they reported. The hadith were recorded 200 years after Mohammed's death, so there is a long chain of who said what to whom.

jihad, struggle, also fighting in the path of Allah. It is much more than killing or war. All effort for the supremacy of Islam is included. Writing a letter to the editor about Islam, making demands on employers or voting for a Muslim candidate are all jihad.

jinn, a conscious being on earth, made of fire. They can work for good or bad. The Koran says that some of them are Muslims.

jizya, a special tax on kafirs in Islamic countries. In history texts it is called a poll tax and can be as high as 50% of the income.

Kabah, a stone building, cubic in shape, measuring about 30 feet on edge. The Black Stone is mounted in a corner. There is no Islam without the Kabah.

kafir, a nonbeliever, a non-Muslim. The lowest form of life, cursed by Allah

mullah, an Islamic religious leader of the Shia sect.

poll tax, a tax per person, also known as jizya, that is paid by dhimmis. It can be as high as 50% of income.

prostrations, lowering yourself to the ground while praying, part of Islamic prayer.

Quraysh, Mohammed's tribe.

rightly guided caliphs, the first four caliphs—Abu Bakr, Umar, Uthman and Ali. They were very close to Mohammed.

Saed, one of Mohammed's close companions. He gave the judgment that lead to the beheading of 800 male Jews.

Safiya, a Jewess who married Mohammed after he killed her husband, cousin and tortured her father to death.

Sharia, Islamic law based upon the Koran, Sira and Hadith. In it all kafirs are second class citizens, at best. Islam has the goal of replacing our Constitution with Sharia law.

Shia, those who follow Ali, about 10% of Muslims, strong in Iran and southern Iraq. The differences between the Shia and the Sunni are mainly political. They willing to kill each other, but are united against the kafirs.

spirit, the archangel Gabriel.

Sunni, those who follow the Sunna. They are about 90% of Muslims. The difference between Sunni and Shia is mainly political and is over who can be caliph.

Sunna, what Mohammed did and said is called the Sunna. It is the ideal pattern of Islamic life.

sura, a chapter of the Koran.

Sira, the life of Mohammed by Ishaq, *Sirat Rasul Allah.* It is one of Islam's three sacred texts, the Trilogy.

Sufism, a mystical form of Islam. It was adopted from Hinduism and Buddhism by conquered kafirs who converted to Islam.

Torah, the first five books of the Old Testament.

Trilogy, the three sacred texts of Islam—the Koran, the Sira (Mohammed's biography) and the Hadith (what Mohammed did and said).

Umar, the second caliph. He created the Islamic empire.

umma, the Muslim political, religious and cultural community. A Muslim is a member of the umma, before his is a citizen.

Uthman, the third caliph, a close companion of Mohammed. He was assassinated by Muslims.

zakat, a tax on Muslims, one of the Five Pillars. It is usually 2.5% of wealth.

Printed in the United States
125507LV00006B/79-81/P